top down
reimagining set-in sleeve design

by Elizabeth Doherty

with Quince & Co

contents

adjustments and fitting

addenda

foreword

Knitting a sweater from the neck down isn't new. Barbara Walker wrote her revolutionary book *Knitting from the Top* in 1972. But working a sweater upside down didn't become popular until recently. The method has much to recommend it: Walker's classic top-down raglan sweater is worked in the round (no seaming); the crucial fitting stage takes place early, at the neckline and shoulders, when ripping out involves fewer stitches than it would if the piece were knitted bottom up; you can fit your piece as you go, trying it on at various stages in its evolution and making adjustments as needed; and lengths of sleeves and body can be determined at the end, no guesswork involved.

Advantages aside, not everyone wants a raglan sweater. Some prefer the tailored look of a sweater with a classic set-in sleeve. Although Barbara Walker describes a method for working a top-down set-in sleeve sweater in her book, the result in the crucial shoulder and cap area, where fit and ease need to work together to gracefully cover the round angle of the shoulder, wasn't always as handsome and tidy as one might wish.

Elizabeth Doherty, fan of both top-down knitting and set-in sleeve structure, has, through painstaking experiment, tweaked Walker's basic picked-up set-in sleeve method to create perfect seamless sleeve caps that look and fit as nicely as any knitted from the cuff up. In this book she explains her approach and demonstrates it in six patterns for knitted-from-the-shoulder sweaters. In addition, she explains how best to deal with individual fitting issues and offers strategies on how to pick up and knit a perfectly fitting cap in any armhole you might encounter, be it tall and narrow or short and wide.

If you like to knit seamlessly and love a set-in sleeve, this book is your best guide to making a beautiful sweater.

Pam Allen

a sleeve journey

When it comes to sweater knitting, I have a strong preference for top-down construction. In working a sweater from the top, you can fit as you go, making it easy to customize the yoke depth, as well as the length of body and sleeves. And the commitment level is lower. You begin with many fewer stitches, so if the size you've chosen to make is not quite right, you'll probably know it by the time you've knitted just a few inches, and starting over is far less painful.

That said, I have an even stronger preference for classic, pieced designs with set-in sleeves. I think this style of sweater is universally flattering—it looks great on most people because it emphasizes the vertical lines of the wearer's body, rather than creating style lines that run counter to the human form. And the more anatomical fit provided by a set-in sleeve allows for a full range of movement with a minimum of excess fabric.

I'm also a big fan of the structure that seams give to a garment. The small bit of reinforcement provided by a shoulder seam can make a huge difference in how a sweater hangs on the body. Likewise, the seams between the sleeves and the body of the sweater provide a strong, flexible join in an area that receives a lot of stress, and they add structure to the framework that holds the sleeve, helping it to hang smoothly. All in all, the classic set-in sleeve sweater is a beautiful thing. The only problem is that it is generally knitted bottom-up.

design exercise

Now, I live in a really hilly place. I ride my bike whenever I can, and when I'm grinding up a long hill, it helps to have a diversion—something to keep me from focusing on my legs. A complex design problem is just the thing. On one such ride a few years back I thought 'Why not just turn it all around?' and spent the rest of that ride, and several more, reconstructing the classic set-in sleeve design from the top down.

I could easily picture how to knit the body…I'd cast on at the shoulders, work the upper back, then go back to the cast-on edge at each shoulder and pick up stitches for the fronts. I'd work them to the same depth, join fronts and back together, and then, zoom! the body could be worked in one piece all the way to the hem.

The sleeves were more challenging. If you simply pick up stitches around an armhole and start knitting, you'll wind up with a cylinder that sticks out at a right angle to the sweater body. Not really ideal. If you want a sleeve that actually slants toward the floor like the human arm, a sleeve cap is needed.

A true set-in sleeve cap is a little piece of engineering magic. By means of some clever shaping, a flat piece of fabric is turned into a complex three-dimensional form. It's not easy to visualize making such a shape in the round, and top-down, but Barbara Walker's groundbreaking 1972 book, *Knitting from the Top,* provided a place to start.

Here then, was the road map for my top-down design. The journey it set me on led, ultimately, toward a much deeper exploration of the remarkable sleeve cap. I'm happy to share with you some of the many things I learned along the way.

But as much as this book has to say about sleeves, in the end it's really about making sweaters that fit you in the right places. There are six designs here, all knit from the top. Be sure to read the section on fitting first, but if you prefer to skip the theory and go straight to the practice, I invite you to dive right in.

set-in sleeve basics

the top-down sweater body

Working from the top has some decided benefits for set-in sleeve garments. You begin by fitting the sweater to the frame of your shoulders—the critical fit area for set-in sleeves. Once the upper bodice fits you properly, you can immediately see where adjustments are needed, whether to suit your body, or your personal style.

For a good fit with this style of sweater, you want a back neckline that dips slightly lower than the shoulder seams. This keeps the neckline edge from impinging on the neck vertebrae, making it more comfortable to wear. And because it allows the shoulder seams to take more of the weight of the garment, it helps the sweater to hang properly.

You therefore begin the sweater body by casting on a separate piece for each back shoulder. Next, a few short rows are worked, creating a wedge of fabric that angles the shoulder piece so it sits nicely on the shoulder slope. Stitches are then cast on between the two pieces, uniting them to form the upper back.

The back is worked straight, then increases are made at each edge of the piece, shaping the curved sides of the lower armhole. When the underarm depth has been reached, the back stitches are placed on hold, and the work

is turned 180° so that the cast-on edges of the shoulders are uppermost.

Here stitches are picked up along one cast-on edge for a front. In a cardigan, the right front comes first. It is worked to the underarm, with shaping as for the back, and placed on hold. The left front is then worked in the same manner. For a pullover, the left front shoulder is worked first to the depth of the neckline. The right front shoulder is then worked to an equal depth, then stitches are cast on between the front pieces to form the neckline. From there the single front piece is continued to the underarms.

This sequence creates a smooth transition for joining fronts to back. On the next right side row, stitches are cast on between each section, completing the underarm shaping and joining the body in one piece. At this point, the full bust circumference, less the width of any button bands, is on the needles.

From here to the hem, the body is knit in one piece. As it progresses, you'll try on your sweater and make decisions about the position of shaping decreases and increases, or length, in response to how it actually fits.

new to short rows?

This handy technique is used in top-down sweater construction to selectively add fabric to shoulders, sleeve caps, and even neckline edges. If you are unfamiliar with short row shaping, not to worry, you'll find a detailed explanation on page 68.

With this top-down method, it's easy see how you can produce a sweater body that's similar in every respect to one that's been knit from the bottom up, by simply reversing all the steps. But to understand how to replicate the classic sleeve cap from the top, it will help to first understand how a set-in sleeve actually works.

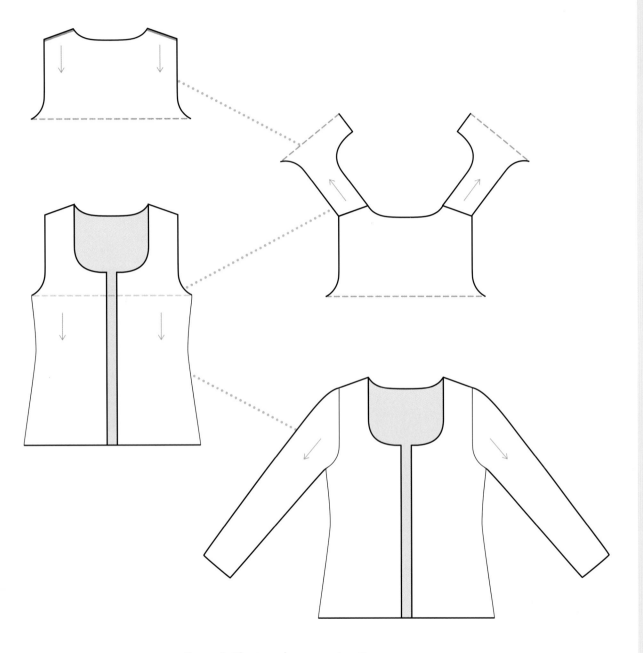

Figure 1. The top-down construction sequence

about row gauge

There is one difference to be aware of when knitting a sweater from the top, and that's the importance of row gauge when shaping the armhole.

In a bottom-up design, when you knit the upper bodice, you work the underarm shaping first, then you are usually instructed to 'work as established' until the armhole reaches a certain depth.

When working from the top, the underarm shaping is worked *after* the upper bodice has been knit to a specified depth. If you are following the pattern's row counts and your row gauge is different from the pattern's stated gauge, it can affect the depth of your armhole and, in turn, the fit of your sleeve.

For this reason, the patterns in this book provide depth measurements at various points in the shaping of the upper bodice. As you work, keep an eye on those measurements. If you need to make an adjustment for a row gauge difference, you'll find advice on page 104.

sleeve cap mechanics

A set-in sleeve cap is an extraordinarily complex form. It's a truncated cylinder with a slightly curved top—kind of like a macaroni elbow that's been sliced off at an angle. Many knitters, and even a few engineers I know, have trouble visualizing the subtle interplay of geometries that combine to create this shape—especially when viewed in three dimensions. By looking at a traditional sleeve cap, worked flat, we'll be better able to see the shapes we need to create to successfully turn it upside-down.

the elements of fit

Since a garment's armhole provides the framework for the sleeve cap, the logical starting point for creating a great-fitting sleeve is with an armhole that's properly sized for the wearer, and properly positioned relative to the wearer's cross-shoulder width.

In general terms, this means that it should fit as close as is possible to the underarm while still providing a comfortable fit, and that the edge of the armhole should align vertically with the point where the shoulder articulates. We'll look at both of these ideas in more depth later.

Next, the sleeve cap itself needs contours that match the body's (Figure 2). A little extra fabric is needed in the upper cap, so that it fits the curve of the shoulder without pulling or straining. For the truncated cylinder right below this, the mid cap, much less fabric is needed for a smooth fit. In the lower cap, excess fabric must be carved away so that the sleeve fits into the curved bottom of the armhole smoothly and doesn't bunch under the arm.

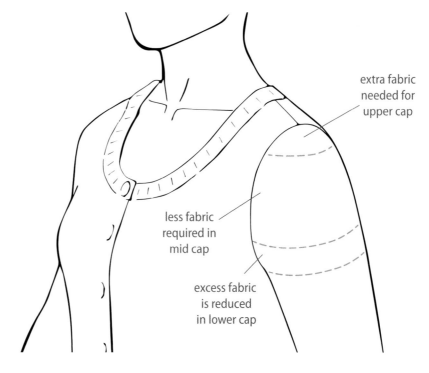

extra fabric needed for upper cap

less fabric required in mid cap

excess fabric is reduced in lower cap

Figure 2. The set-in sleeve cap

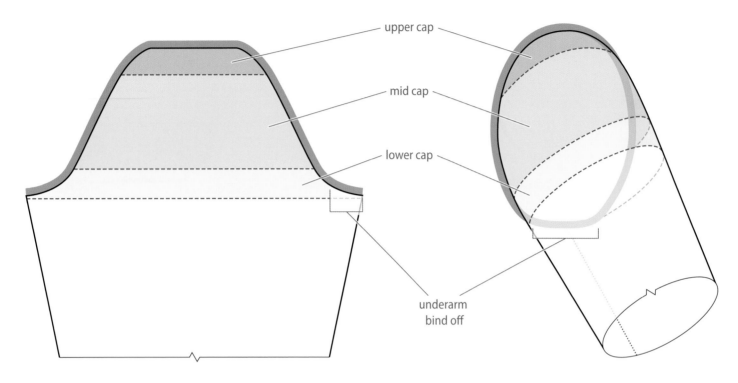

upper cap

mid cap

lower cap

underarm
bind off

Figure 3. Parts of the sleeve cap

the classic set-in sleeve

In a bottom-up set-in sleeve design, the body of the garment is cast on at the hem and worked—either in pieces or all in one piece—to the armholes, then a group of stitches is bound off all at once to form the underarm. This bind-off is analogous to the stitches cast on at the underarm when joining fronts to back in a sweater body worked from the top down. After the initial bind-off, subsequent groups of stitches may be bound off to shape the lower curve of the armhole, then single-stitch decreases are made along the sides of the armhole to decrease the piece's width to the desired measurement. This also corresponds to the shaping increases made to the armhole when working from the top.

The bottom-up sleeve is cast on at the cuff and worked to the underarm. Here, groups of stitches are bound off on each side of the sleeve to quickly carve away fabric, reducing bulk under the arms. The number of stitches bound off at the underarm will match the corresponding bind-off on the body (Figure 3). After this first bind-off, smaller groups of stitches may be bound off on each side to shape the lower sleeve cap. Again this will match the shaping on the body.

From this point, stitches are decreased at a slower rate to taper the cap towards the shoulder. The upper cap may be decreased at a faster rate to taper the edges more quickly, then the

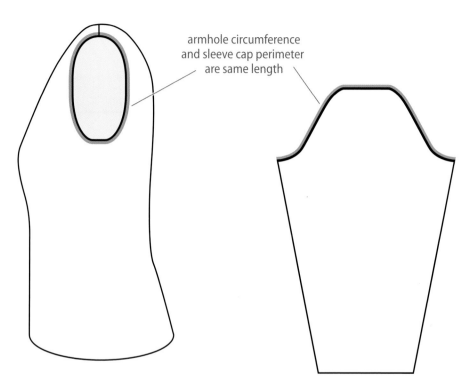

armhole circumference
and sleeve cap perimeter
are same length

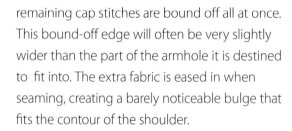

Figure 4. Fitting the cap

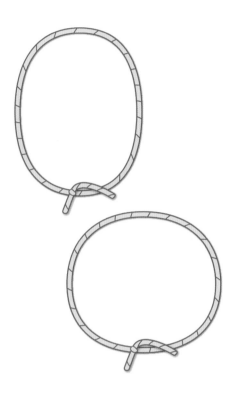

Figure 5. Same length, different shape

remaining cap stitches are bound off all at once. This bound-off edge will often be very slightly wider than the part of the armhole it is destined to fit into. The extra fabric is eased in when seaming, creating a barely noticeable bulge that fits the contour of the shoulder.

fitting the cap to the body

In many areas of knitting there is latitude for fudging things a bit. The stretchy nature of knit-ted fabric can forgive some slight differences. Not so in fitting the sleeve cap to the armhole. Here, the critical business lies in matching the length of the outside perimeter of the sleeve cap to the circumference of the armhole.

Imagine measuring around the curved edge of the armhole opening with a flexible tape mea-sure. Now picture running your tape along the arching top of the sleeve cap. For the sleeve cap to fit smoothly into the body of the sweater, these two measurements must be the same, or nearly the same (Figure 4).

As noted above, a small amount of extra fabric in the sleeve cap, say ¼" [1 cm] or less, may be de-sirable to accommodate the shoulder curve. This extra fabric is eased in when the sweater is made up. But if the cap's perimeter is much larger than the armhole opening, the excess fabric will result in a puffed sleeve cap. If much smaller, the body of the sweater may pucker when the sleeve is

17

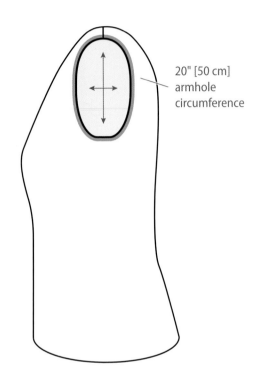

20" [50 cm]
armhole
circumference

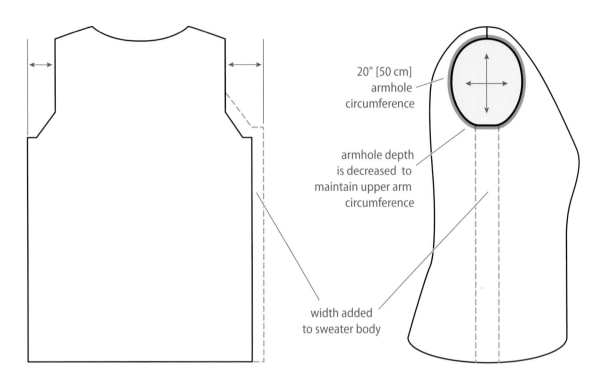

20" [50 cm]
armhole
circumference

armhole depth
is decreased to
maintain upper arm
circumference

width added
to sweater body

Figure 6. The link between armhole depth and width

sewn in, and the top of the cap will pull against the shoulder curve.

armhole shape and cap depth

The key thing to understand about set-in sleeves is that two armholes with the same overall circumference may be shaped very differently. To picture this, tie a piece of string into a circle. You'll see right away that the same length of string can be pushed into various oval shapes (Figure 5).

One may be shallow and wide, the other long and narrow, but the length of the string does not change at all.

A set-in sleeve sweater that's designed to fit with minimal ease at the bust will usually have a relatively long and narrow armhole. To understand why, look at the garment laid out flat. The cross-shoulder width and bust width are fixed measurements, and the width of the armhole is the difference between those two measure-

ments. If you keep the shoulder width the same, and add width to the body of the garment, the armhole opening will become wider. So in order to maintain the same circumference it must also become shallower (Figure 6).

Changing the aspect ratio of the armhole also affects the shape of the sleeve cap that fits into that opening (Figure 7). A long and narrow armhole will need a cap with the same proportions. A shallow, wide opening will likewise need

18

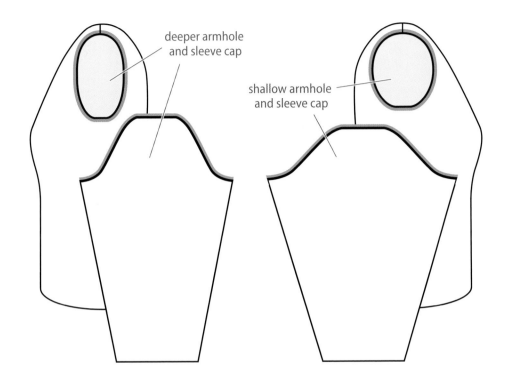

Figure 7. Armhole shape and cap depth

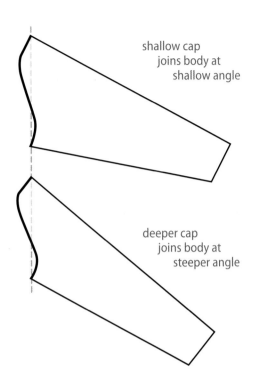

Figure 8. Cap depth and sleeve angles

a wide and shallow cap. Further, the shape of the armhole and sleeve cap will in turn affect the angle at which the sleeve joins the body, and from there, the fit of the sleeve proper.

cap depth and sleeve fit

If you look at the arched shape of a sleeve cap laid out flat, it can be very difficult to see what role cap depth plays in the fit of the sleeve—but fold it in half and rotate it so that the curved edge is more or less vertical, and you'll start to get the picture (Figure 8).

A wide shallow cap will join the body at a shallower angle, providing greater mobility, but will have a bit more fabric under the arms. A shallow cap is typically found in garments with larger amounts of positive ease in the body, such as in heavy outerwear sweaters, and in men's and children's garments, or in sweaters designed with an oversized fit in the body.

A long, narrow sleeve cap will join the sweater body at a steeper angle, providing a sleeker fit. This is the cap most often used in classic-fitting women's sweaters that have minimal positive ease through the bust.

Now that we understand the logic behind sleeve cap shaping, let's apply it to making a top-down sleeve that fits perfectly.

sleeves from the top

Although the classic, bottom-up set-in sleeve sets the standard for great fit, in practice, many knitters struggle with getting them right. Sewing a sleeve into the armhole can be tricky. Getting the sleeve length right when working from the cuff up can also be an issue. But these are minor difficulties. The greatest challenge when working bottom-up is that adjusting the fit of the sleeve cap is very, very difficult. If you make even minor changes to the armhole width or depth, the upper arm width, or the cap depth, the delicate balance between the cap perimeter and armhole circumference can be thrown off. For this reason, most knitters will settle for a less-than-perfect fit—often an upper bodice that is far too wide for the wearer's shoulders—rather than take on sleeve cap and armhole alterations.

With a top-down set-in sleeve, many of those challenges are eliminated. There's no sewing—the stitches are picked up around the armhole, creating a firm and flexible join between the sweater body and the sleeve that can be superior to a sewn seam.

Picking up stitches also means that there is just one selvedge, so there is half the bulk at the join. This can make a big difference in the appearance of the seam when working with yarns at the heavier end of the spectrum. And working from the top makes adjustments to the

length of the sleeve simple. But best of all, it is much, much easier to adjust the fit of the upper bodice, armhole and sleeve cap.

the top-down process

Any top-down set-in sleeve begins by picking up stitches around the armhole of a completed sweater body. The body may be worked bottom-up, top-down, in pieces, or seamlessly—it really doesn't matter, as long the armholes have the classic set-in shape, with vertical sides and a curved underarm.

With a traditional bottom-up sleeve cap, the art of achieving a perfect fit lies in finessing the rate and number of decreases from the full sleeve width at the upper arm to the upper cap bind-off, so that the length of the cap perimeter matches the circumference of the armhole opening. The depth of the sleeve cap is a critical part of the shaping equation, since it is tied directly to the rate of decrease for the cap.

In a top-down sleeve cap, it is the way in which the stitches are picked up, and the manner in which the short rows are worked, that determines the fit of the cap into the armhole opening—and the fit of the sleeve to your shoulder and arm. The depth of the cap is still important to the overall shape, but it is something of a by-product of the process of working the cap.

the improved top-down sleeve

If you begin with the idea of recreating all of the clever shaping found in the classic bottom-up sleeve cap, it's surprisingly easy to make a top-down cap that fits really well. Here's how it works:

Start the pick-up round at the upper cap

When you pick up stitches on a garment, in most cases you begin at an edge or seam. But for a sleeve that will be shaped with short rows, you want to keep the short row wraps as unobtrusive as possible—so it's preferable to have them sit directly against the join between sleeve and body.

For this reason, the sleeve pick-up round begins with the stitches that will form the first short row pair of the upper cap. By starting at the point where that pair will end, (let's call this point the *first terminus*), each new stitch that gets wrapped will be a fresh stitch from the pick-up round. Butting the short row wraps up against the sleeve join also makes it possible to leave the wraps in place, rather than picking them up. This simplifies the process, creates a firmer join, and gives a nice clean look to the sleeve.

So how do you know where to start the pick-up round if you don't begin at an edge or seam? Here's the secret: the width of the first short row should be approximately 20% of the desired sleeve circumference at the upper arm. This will create a smooth, comfortable arc that matches the curve of the shoulder. So, for example, with a 13" [33 cm] sleeve, the ideal width for the first short row would be approximately 2½" [6.5 cm]. This width will be centered on the shoulder, so

the pick-up round would begin 1¼" [3.25 cm] to the right of the shoulder seam.

Vary the pick-up rate around the armhole

Different amounts of fabric are required for each part of the sleeve cap. With this in mind, you can actually begin contouring the cap as you pick up stitches around the armhole. In the upper cap, extra fullness is needed to accommodate the curve of the shoulder. Picking up 85–90% of the

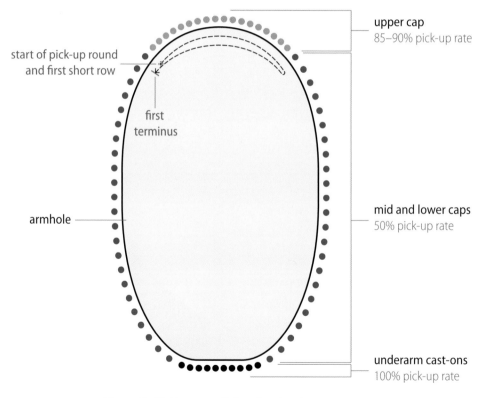

start of pick-up round and first short row

first terminus

armhole

upper cap
85–90% pick-up rate

mid and lower caps
50% pick-up rate

underarm cast-ons
100% pick-up rate

Figure 9. Picking up stitches for the sleeve cap

available stitches will add the needed ease. Continuing the example, if there were 16 rows in that 2½" [6.5 cm] width, you'd pick up 14 stitches.

In the mid and lower caps, the sides of the sleeve cap join the body of the sweater at an angle. Each stitch actually covers a bit more territory than it would in a perpendicular join, and many fewer stitches are needed.

Approximately 50% of the available stitches are picked up throughout this section—many more than this and the sleeve fabric may pucker and puff, any fewer and it will gap. So if there were 40 rows between the upper cap and the cast-on stitches at the underarm, you'd pick up 20 stitches on each side. In practice, you'll often need 1 or 2 extras on each side for a smooth pick-up round, so let's call it 22 stitches for each side.

At the very bottom of the armhole, where stitches have been cast on for shaping and joining, 100% of the available stitches—or 1 stitch for every cast-on stitch—are picked up.

This creates a smooth join in an area that receives a lot of stress and ensures that the sleeve fits the underarm snugly without pulling or straining at the stitches. If there were 2 stitches cast on at each side of the armhole for the underarm shaping, and 4 stitches cast on while joining fronts and back, you'd pick up 8 stitches in the bottom of the underarm.

The total number of stitches picked up with this method will be greater than the number of stitches required at the upper arm, but the extras will be decreased when the lower cap is shaped. You've now picked up 66 stitches around the armhole. By the time your sleeve cap reaches the upper arm, that number will have been reduced to achieve your desired sleeve circumference.

Build the upper cap

When the stitches have been picked up all the way around the armhole and back to the starting point, the cap shaping begins. An initial short row is worked across the closely-spaced upper cap stitches to the first mid cap stitch. A wrap-and-turn is made, and the row worked back to the starting point. The next stitch is wrapped and the work turned back to the right side.

Now the upper cap is feathered into the mid cap by working an extra stitch between each short row turn for a few rows. This results in a more gradual curve at the top of the cap, rounding out any potential 'corners'.

Angle the mid cap more steeply

In the mid cap, the short-row turns are made each time a previously unworked stitch is encountered. Working the wrap-and-turns successively, with no extra stitches in between, adds width to the sleeve more quickly, and results in a much steeper join between the cap and the body.

Contour the lower cap

In the lower armhole, just before the underarm cast-on stitches are reached, decreases are made, eliminating excess fabric under the arm. Two stitches are wrapped together at the same time, then knit or purled together the next time they are encountered. These twin-wrap decreases contour the sleeve closer to the underarm, while keeping the join between body and sleeve free of gaps or puckers. This provides the same kind of shaping for the underarm that is achieved in a bottom-up cap by binding off groups of stitches.

Join in the round

When the lower cap decreases are complete, a final set of short rows is worked. The sleeve is then joined in the round and worked to the desired length. Decreases to shape the sleeve are begun a few rounds after the sleeve is joined in the round. When the first decrease round has been worked, the desired stitch count for the biceps measurement plus ease will have been reached.

et voilá!

If you start with a well-fitting armhole and follow these steps, you'll have a sleeve cap that fits like a classic bottom-up sleeve cap. Best of all, adjustments are generally made to the armhole first, rather than to the actual sleeve cap. If you try on your sweater as you go, you'll know in advance that your set-in sleeve will fit.

fitting a set-in sleeve sweater

For many parts of a garment, fit is a purely subjective thing. You may prefer your sweaters to have negative ease through the bust and a loose figure-skimming fit throughout the rest of the body. You may like a looser fit all over, or hate it when a sweater doesn't hug your hips. These are all matters of personal preference. There is one place, however, where fit and ease are not subjective, and that's the shoulders.

For a set-in sleeve garment to hang properly on your body, the vertical line of the armhole should line up with the protruding bump at the end of each shoulder known as the *acromial process* (Figure 10). There's a little leeway here, but basically, if the armhole seam falls too far to the outside of this bump, the sleeves will droop and the whole sweater will feel sloppy. Too far inside and you will definitely feel squeezed, and the garment will look too small—no matter how much positive ease there is in the rest of it.

This means that for a top-down set-in sleeve sweater, the logical place to start when choosing a size to knit is with your cross-shoulder width.

by the numbers

To find your cross-shoulder width, stand up straight with your arms at your sides and shoulders back. Have a friend draw an imaginary line straight down from each *acromial process* to the fold of skin where the arms join the body and measure the width between these lines across your back. Then have them measure the same distance across the front.

For most of us, especially those who work at computers (or knit!), the cross-front width will be a bit smaller than the cross-back width. I generally use the smaller, front width when selecting a size, because the knitted fabric will stretch to accommodate a slightly wider back measurement, but it won't shrink to fit

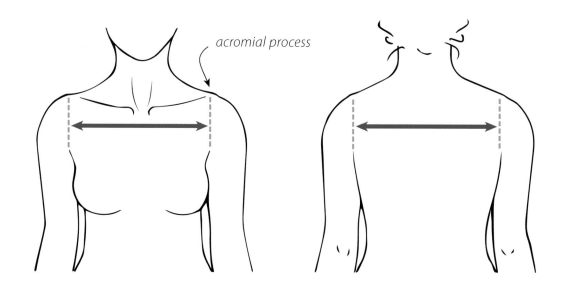

acromial process

Figure 10. Cross-shoulder width

a narrower one. You can use whichever measurement makes more sense to you, or average them and use that number.

Once you've decided on your best shoulder measurement, check it against the pattern's schematic for your sweater. Find the size whose cross-shoulder measurement comes closest to your own.

This is size that you will cast on.

So far, so good. Now have your friend take your measurements at the fullest part of the upper arm, bust and hips. For the hip measurement, refer to your pattern's schematic for the overall garment length, and measure your hip circumference at the widest point that falls within that

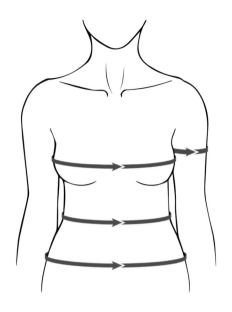

Figure 11. Circumferential measurements

length. And finally, measure the circumference at the narrowest part of your torso.

Decide how much ease you'd like the sweater to have in these key areas (see *'About ease'*, below), and add or subtract it from the measurements you've taken. Compare the results to the measurements on the schematic for the size you've chosen, and note any changes that may be needed.

If your bust and hip measurements don't align with the pattern's cross-shoulder width, or the length and ease aren't to your taste, not to worry. We'll look at modifying the pattern to tailor it to your shape in *'Adjusting fit'*, beginning on page 106.

about ease

Simply stated, ease is the difference in circumference between a given body part and the garment that's covering it. If a sweater is larger in circumference than its wearer, it is said to have positive ease, if smaller, negative ease.

In practice though, it's rarely that simple. More often, different amounts of ease are used in different areas of the garment. A sweater may have negative ease in the bust and positive ease elsewhere. And even if negative ease is preferred in the entire body

of the sweater, a little positive ease is almost always desirable in the sleeves.

■ Ease preferences vary greatly by individual. What is comfortable to one wearer may feel sausage-tight to another.

■ Ease can also be affected by the weight of the yarn. Measurements for sweaters are taken on the outside of the garment, but you need to fit into the inside. The bulkier your yarn, the smaller the interior of the garment is, so more ease is required

to get the same fit in a bulky garment than in one worked at a fine gauge.

■ Perceived ease can be affected by the garment's fabric. The same yarn worked at a loose gauge may be comfortable with less ease than it would be if worked at a firmer gauge. Likewise a garment in an all-over lace pattern may require less ease than one in stockinette, or with lots of cables.

Find garments in your closet that fit as you prefer, and let them guide your choices about ease.

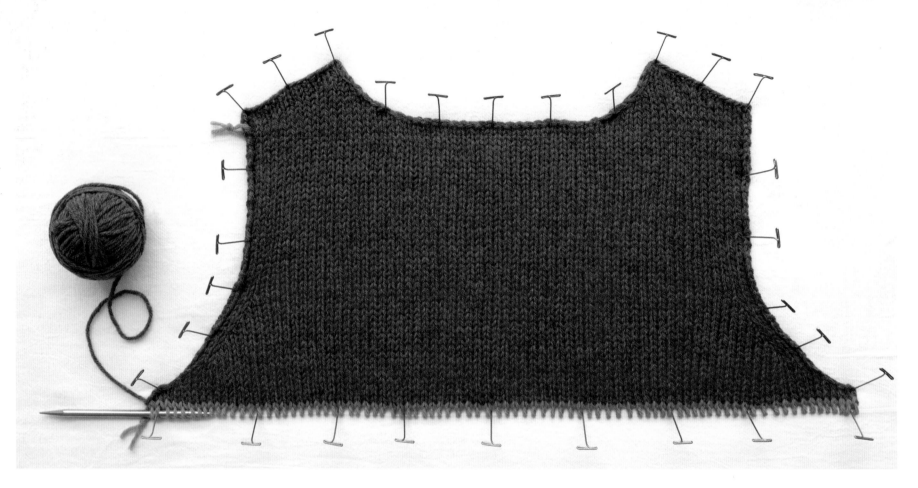

blocking on the needles

As your sweater progresses, if you have any concerns about the size you've chosen or about gauge, stop and wet block it.

First, be sure to read about measuring and evaluating a swatch, on pages 102 and 103. Next, leaving the working yarn attached, knit a couple of rows using waste yarn. The waste yarn rows will support that last row of garment stitches,

preventing a line from forming between the blocked and unblocked work.

If you are using wood or bamboo needles, slip your stitches temporarily to a metal needle, then soak and block the piece just as if it was a swatch, gently patting out or pinning as needed. Don't be concerned if you see a bit of dye in the water. That free dye should be consistent across the dye lot—you won't wind up with a lighter patch.

When the work is dry, unpin it, shake it out, and let it rest a bit. Check the shoulder width by holding it against yourself to be sure that you've got the right size cast on. Double-check the row gauge, too, to see whether you need to adjust the number of rows for the armhole.

Once you've verified your size and noted any adjustments, zip out the waste yarn, put your stitches back on the needles, and get back to work!

26

the sweaters

sans serif

serif

underwood

meris

copperplate

clarendon

sans serif ~Sport~

This is the classic set-in-sleeve cardigan, updated with a deeper neckline and flattering waist shaping. Horizontal braids provide a crisp, linear, contrast for the simple ribbed edgings. Free-hanging pocket linings are worked in fingering-weight Finch to reduce bulk.

Sans Serif is designed to serve as a template for knitting the classic set-in-sleeve cardigan from the top down. Work it as written—or change materials for the skirt, as with Serif, page 50. Change the edgings. Add stripes or a cable. Have fun and make the design your own!

Finished measurements

Shoulder width: 12¼ (12¾, 13¼, 13¾, 14½, 15, 16, 17, 17½, 18)" [31 (32.5, 33.5, 34.5, 37, 38, 40.5, 43, 44, 45.5) cm]

Bust circumference: 30 (33, 35¾, 38½, 42¼, 45¼, 47½, 50¼, 53¼, 57)" [76.5 (83.5, 91, 98, 107.5, 114.5, 120.5, 128, 135, 144.5) cm]

Sample shown in 13¾" [34.5 cm] shoulder, 38½" [98 cm] bust size.

Suggested ease at bust: -1 to +1" [-2.5 to +2.5 cm]

Materials
Yarn   ~DK~

Lark by Quince & Co.
(100% American wool; 134 yd [123 m] / 50 g)

• 8 (8, 9, 9, 10, 11, 12, 12, 13, 14) skeins Kittywake (151)

Finch by Quince & Co.
(100% American wool; 221 yd [202 m] / 50 g)

• 1 skein Kittywake (151)

Needles

Body
• US 9 [5.5 mm] circ, 32" [80 cm] long or longer
• US 7 [4.5 mm] circ, 32" [80 cm] long or longer

Sleeves
• US 9 [5.5 mm] circ, 16" [40 cm] long
• US 9 [5.5 mm] needles of preferred style for working small circumferences in the round
• US 5 [3.75 mm] circ, 24" [60 cm] long, for picking up stitches
• US 5 [3.75 mm] needles of preferred style for working small circumferences in the round

Bands
• US 3 [3.25 mm] circ, 32" [80 cm] long
• US 5 [3.75 mm] circ, 32" [80 cm] long

Or size to obtain gauge

Notions
• Waste yarn of similar gauge and contrasting color
• Stitch markers, both removable and fixed ring, including one unique
• 6 buttons, 13⁄16" [20 mm] in diameter
• Yarn needle

Gauge
17 sts and 26 rows = 4" [10 cm] in stockinette stitch, worked flat, on US 9 [5.5 mm] needles, after blocking.

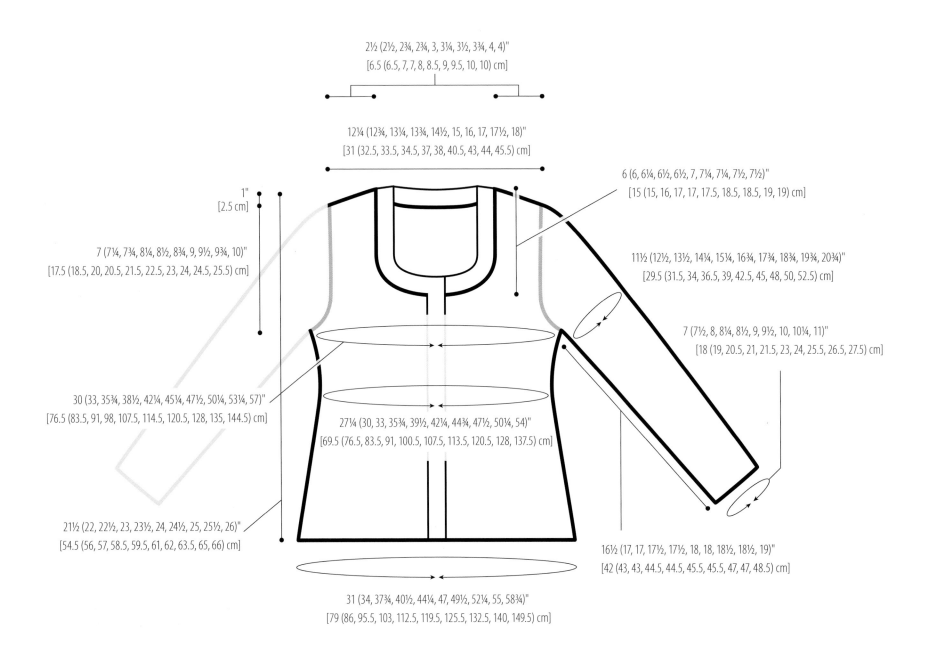

2½ (2½, 2¾, 2¾, 3, 3¼, 3½, 3¾, 4, 4)"
[6.5 (6.5, 7, 7, 8, 8.5, 9, 9.5, 10, 10) cm]

12¼ (12¾, 13¼, 13¾, 14½, 15, 16, 17, 17½, 18)"
[31 (32.5, 33.5, 34.5, 37, 38, 40.5, 43, 44, 45.5) cm]

6 (6, 6¼, 6½, 6½, 7, 7¼, 7¼, 7½, 7½)"
[15 (15, 16, 17, 17, 17.5, 18.5, 18.5, 19, 19) cm]

1"
[2.5 cm]

7 (7¼, 7¾, 8¼, 8½, 8¾, 9, 9½, 9¾, 10)"
[17.5 (18.5, 20, 20.5, 21.5, 22.5, 23, 24, 24.5, 25.5) cm]

11½ (12½, 13½, 14¼, 15¼, 16¾, 17¾, 18¾, 19¾, 20¾)"
[29.5 (31.5, 34, 36.5, 39, 42.5, 45, 48, 50, 52.5) cm]

7 (7½, 8, 8¼, 8½, 9, 9½, 10, 10¼, 11)"
[18 (19, 20.5, 21, 21.5, 23, 24, 25.5, 26.5, 27.5) cm]

30 (33, 35¾, 38½, 42¼, 45¼, 47½, 50¼, 53¼, 57)"
[76.5 (83.5, 91, 98, 107.5, 114.5, 120.5, 128, 135, 144.5) cm]

27¼ (30, 33, 35¾, 39½, 42¼, 44¾, 47½, 50¼, 54)"
[69.5 (76.5, 83.5, 91, 100.5, 107.5, 113.5, 120.5, 128, 137.5) cm]

21½ (22, 22½, 23, 23½, 24, 24½, 25, 25½, 26)"
[54.5 (56, 57, 58.5, 59.5, 61, 62, 63.5, 65, 66) cm]

16½ (17, 17, 17½, 17½, 18, 18, 18½, 18½, 19)"
[42 (43, 43, 44.5, 44.5, 45.5, 45.5, 47, 47, 48.5) cm]

31 (34, 37¾, 40½, 44¼, 47, 49½, 52¼, 55, 58¾)"
[79 (86, 95.5, 103, 112.5, 119.5, 125.5, 132.5, 140, 149.5) cm]

BACK (begin at right shoulder)

With US 9 [5.5 mm] circ and the long-tail cast-on, loosely CO 13 (13, 14, 14, 15, 16, 17, 18, 19, 19) sts with main yarn.

Set-up row: (WS) P1, k1, purl to end.

Shape right shoulder

Short Row 1: (RS) K3 (3, 3, 3, 3, 3, 4, 4, 4, 4), w&t; (WS) purl to end.

Short Row 2: (RS) K1, RLI, knit to wrapped st, pick up wrap, k2 (2, 2, 2, 3, 3, 3, 4, 4, 4), w&t; (WS) purl to end.

Short Row 3: Rep Short Row 2.

Row 4: (RS) Cable CO 3 sts, knit to last 2 sts, picking up prev wrap, p1, k1—18 (18, 19, 19, 20, 21, 22, 23, 24, 24) sts.

Row 5: P1, k1, purl to end.

Break yarn and slip stitches onto waste yarn.

Left shoulder

With US 9 [5.5 mm] circ, loosely CO 13 (13, 14, 14, 15, 16, 17, 18, 19, 19) sts.

Set-up Row 1: (WS) Purl to last 2 sts, k1, p1.

Set-up Row 2: K1, p1, knit to end.

Shape left shoulder

Short Row 1: (WS) P3 (3, 3, 3, 3, 3, 4, 4, 4, 4), w&t; (RS) knit to last st, LLI, k1.

Short Row 2: (WS) Purl to wrapped st, pick up wrap, p2 (2, 2, 2, 3, 3, 3, 4, 4, 4), w&t; (RS) knit to last st, LLI, k1.

Short Row 3: (WS) Purl to wrapped st, pick up wrap, p2 (2, 2, 2, 3, 3, 3, 4, 4, 4), w&t; (RS) knit to last st, LLI, k1.

Row 4: Cable CO 3, purl to last 2 sts, picking up prev wrap, k1, p1—18 (18, 19, 19, 20, 21, 22, 23, 24, 24) sts.

Tie a yarn marker around the last stitch of Row 4.

keeping track of rows

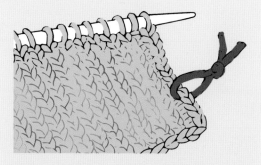

The short rows used to shape the shoulders can make it a little tricky to count rows, so yarn markers are placed, providing a starting point for counting the rows to the underarm shaping. Why use yarn? The soft loops won't distort the edge of your knitting, and are less likely to get confused with other markers.

To make a yarn marker, tie a short length of waste yarn around the base of the specified stitch, and continue working. Snip or untie the yarn marker when no longer needed.

Join shoulders

With RS facing, slip 18 (18, 19, 19, 20, 21, 22, 23, 24, 24) held right shoulder sts to left end of needle holding left shoulder sts.

Left shoulder: (RS) K1, p1, knit to end.

Back neck: Turn work to WS and cable CO 19 (21, 21, 23, 25, 25, 27, 29, 29, 31) sts.

Right shoulder: Turn work to RS. Slip last st cast on back to LH needle, k2tog with first right shoulder st, knit to last 2 sts, p1, k1—54 (56, 58, 60, 64, 66, 70, 74, 76, 78) sts.

Next row: (WS) P1, k1, purl to last 2 sts, k1, p1.

Continue back

Row 1: (RS) K1, p1, knit to last 2 sts, p1, k1.

Row 2: P1, k1, purl to last 2 sts, k1, p1.

Rep Rows 1 and 2 until 36 (36, 36, 36, 34, 34, 36, 38, 36, 36) rows have been worked from yarn marker. Piece should measure approx 6 (6, 6, 6, 5¾, 5¾, 6, 6¼, 6, 6)" [15.5 (15.5, 15.5, 15.5, 14.5, 14.5, 15.5, 16.5, 15.5, 15.5) cm] from cast-on to bottom, measured at armhole edge.

Shape underarms

Next row *inc row:* (RS) K1, p1, k1, RLI, knit to last 3 sts, LLI, k1, p1, k1—2 sts increased.

Next row: P1, k1, purl to last 2 sts, k1, p1.

Rep these two rows 2 (2, 4, 5, 7, 8, 8, 7, 9, 10) more times—60 (62, 68, 72, 80, 84, 88, 90, 96, 100) sts.

Size 30" [76.5 cm]: skip to 'All sizes'
Sizes 33 to 57" [83.5 to 144.5 cm] only:

Next row: (RS) Cable CO – (2, 2, 2, 2, 3, 3, 2, 2, 3) sts, knit to end— – (64, 70, 74, 82, 87, 91, 92, 98, 103) sts.

Next row: Cable CO – (2, 2, 2, 2, 3, 3, 2, 2, 3) sts, purl to end— – (66, 72, 76, 84, 90, 94, 94, 100, 106) sts.

Sizes 33 to 47½" [83.5 to 120.5 cm]: skip to 'All sizes'
Sizes 50¼ to 57" [128 to 144.5 cm] only:

Next row: (RS) Cable CO – (–, –, –, –, –, –, 3, 3, 3) sts, knit to end— – (–, –, –, –, –, –, 97, 103, 109) sts.

Next row: Cable CO – (–, –, –, –, –, –, 3, 3, 3) sts, purl to end— – (–, –, –, –, –, –, 100, 106, 112) sts.

All sizes

Piece should measure approx 7 (7¼, 7¾, 8¼, 8½, 8¾, 9, 9½, 9¾, 10)" [17.5 (18.5, 20, 20.5, 21.5, 22.5, 23, 24, 24.5, 25.5) cm] from cast-on to bottom, measured at armhole edge.

Break yarn and slip stitches onto waste yarn.

FRONTS

Pick up for right front shoulder

With RS facing, attach yarn at armhole edge of right shoulder. With US 9 [5.5 mm] circ, pick up and knit 12 (12, 13, 13, 14, 15, 16, 17, 18, 18) stitches along cast-on edge.

Set-up Row 1: (WS) Purl to last 2 sts, k1, p1.

Set-up Row 2: K1, p1, knit to end.

Shape right shoulder

Short Row 1: (WS) P2 (2, 2, 2, 2, 2, 3, 3, 3, 3), w&t; (RS) knit to end.

Short Row 2: (WS) Purl to wrapped st, pick up wrap, p2 (2, 2, 2, 3, 3, 3, 4, 4, 4), w&t; (RS) knit to end.

Short Row 3: Rep Short Row 2.

Row 4: Purl to last 2 sts, picking up prev wrap, k1, p1.

Tie a yarn marker around the last stitch of Row 4.

Work even for 24 (24, 26, 28, 28, 30, 32, 32, 34, 34) more rows, maintaining purled 'gutter' at armhole edge. Piece should measure approx 4¼ (4¼, 4½, 4¾, 4¾, 5, 5½, 5½, 5¾, 5¾)" [10.5 (10.5, 11.5, 12, 12, 13, 13.5, 13.5, 14.5, 14.5) cm] from shoulder seam to bottom, measured at armhole edge.

Shape right neckline

For some sizes, underarm shaping will begin before neckline shaping is complete. Read ahead to anticipate.

Row 1 *inc row:* (RS) K1, p1, knit to last 2 sts, LLI, k2—13 (13, 14, 14, 15, 16, 17, 18, 19, 19) sts.

Row 2: Purl to last 2 sts, k1, p1.

Row 3: K1, p1, knit to end.

Row 4: Cable CO 2, purl to last 2 sts, k1, p1—15 (15, 16, 16, 17, 18, 19, 20, 21, 21) sts.

Row 5: K1, p1, knit to end.

Row 6: Cable CO 3, purl to last 2 sts, k1, p1—18 (18, 19, 19, 20, 21, 22, 23, 24, 24) sts.

Row 7: K1, p1, knit to end.

Row 8: Cable CO 8 (9, 9, 10, 11, 11, 11, 12, 12, 13), purl to last 2 sts, k1, p1—26 (27, 28, 29, 31, 32, 33, 35, 36, 37) sts.

At the same time, once 36 (36, 36, 36, 34, 34, 36, 38, 36, 36) rows have been worked from yarn marker, begin underarm shaping. Piece should measure approx 6 (6, 6, 6, 5¾, 5¾, 6, 6¼, 6, 6)" [15.5 (15.5, 15.5, 15.5, 14.5, 14.5, 15.5, 16.5, 15.5, 15.5) cm] from shoulder seam to bottom, measured at armhole edge.

Shape right underarm

Next row *inc row:* (RS) K1, p1, k1, RLI, knit to end—1 st increased.

Next row: Purl to last 2 sts, k1, p1.

Rep these two rows 2 (2, 4, 5, 7, 8, 8, 7, 9, 10) more times—29 (30, 33, 35, 39, 41, 42, 43, 46, 48) sts.

Size 30" [76.5 cm]: skip to 'All sizes'
Sizes 33 to 57" [83.5 to 144.5 cm] only:

Next row: (RS) Cable CO – (2, 2, 2, 2, 3, 3, 2, 2, 3) sts, knit to end— – (32, 35, 37, 41, 44, 45, 45, 48, 51) sts.

Next row: Purl.

Sizes 33 to 47½" [83.5 to 120.5 cm]: skip to 'All sizes'
Sizes 50¼ to 57" [128 to 144.5 cm] only:

Next row: (RS) Cable CO – (–, –, –, –, –, –, 3, 3, 3) sts, knit to end— – (–, –, –, –, –, –, 48, 51, 54) sts.

Next row: Purl.

All sizes

Piece should measure approx 7 (7¼, 7¾, 8¼, 8½, 8¾, 9, 9½, 9¾, 10)" [17.5 (18.5, 20, 20.5, 21.5, 22.5, 23, 24, 24.5, 25.5) cm] from shoulder seam to bottom, measured at armhole edge.

Break yarn and slip stitches onto waste yarn.

Pick up for left front shoulder

With RS facing, attach yarn at neck edge of left shoulder. With US 9 [5.5 mm] circ, pick up and knit 12 (12, 13, 13, 14, 15, 16, 17, 18, 18) stitches along cast-on edge.

Set-up row: (WS) P1, k1, purl to end.

Shape left shoulder

Short Row 1: (RS) K2 (2, 2, 2, 2, 2, 3, 3, 3, 3), w&t; (WS) purl to end.

Short Row 2: (RS) Knit to wrapped st, pick up wrap, k2 (2, 2, 2, 3, 3, 3, 4, 4, 4), w&t; (WS) purl to end.

Short Row 3: Rep Short Row 2.

Row 4: Knit to last 2 sts, picking up prev wrap, p1, k1.

Row 5: P1, k1, purl to end.

Tie a yarn marker around the *first* stitch of Row 5, at the armhole edge of piece.

Work even for 24 (24, 26, 28, 28, 30, 32, 32, 34, 34) more rows, maintaining purled 'gutter' at armhole edge. Piece should measure approx 4¼ (4¼, 4½, 4¾, 4¾, 5, 5½, 5½, 5¾, 5¾)" [10.5 (10.5, 11.5, 12, 12, 13, 13.5, 13.5, 14.5, 14.5) cm] from shoulder seam to bottom, measured at armhole edge.

Shape left neckline

For some sizes, underarm shaping will begin before neckline shaping is complete. Read ahead to anticipate.

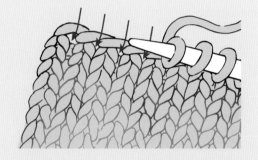

picking up for the fronts

When picking up in the cast-on edge, new stitches are created in the spaces *between* each cast-on stitch. Because of this, there is actually one place less than the number of stitches cast on available for picking up a stitch—so if you've cast on 20 stitches, there are 19 possible stitches to pick up.

To pick up and knit a stitch, insert the needle tip into the V-shaped space between 2 cast on stitches, making sure to go under both strands of the cast-on stitch. Wrap the yarn around the needle as if to knit and pull a loop through—1 stitch picked up.

Row 1 *inc row:* (RS) K2, RLI, knit to last 2 sts, p1, k1—13 (13, 14, 14, 15, 16, 17, 18, 19, 19) sts.

Row 2: P1, k1, purl to end.

Row 3: Cable CO 2, knit to last 2 sts, p1, k1—15 (15, 16, 16, 17, 18, 19, 20, 21, 21) sts.

Row 4: P1, k1, purl to end.

Row 5: Cable CO 3, knit to last 2 sts, p1, k1—18 (18, 19, 19, 20, 21, 22, 23, 24, 24) sts.

Row 6: P1, k1, purl to end. Break yarn, leaving an 8" [20 cm] tail.

Using the long-tail cast-on, CO 9 (10, 10, 11, 12, 12, 12, 13, 13, 14) to the empty end of the needle. With RS facing, sl last CO st to LH needle, and knit it together with the first left front stitch. Work across remaining sts as follows:

Row 7: Knit to last 2 sts, p1, k1—26 (27, 28, 29, 31, 32, 33, 35, 36, 37) sts.

Row 8: P1, k1, purl to end.

At the same time, once 36 (36, 36, 36, 34, 34, 36, 38, 36, 36) rows have been worked from yarn marker, begin underarm shaping. Piece should measure approx 6 (6, 6, 6, 5¾, 5¾, 6, 6¼, 6, 6)" [15.5 (15.5, 15.5, 15.5, 14.5, 14.5, 15.5, 16.5, 15.5, 15.5) cm] from shoulder seam to bottom, measured at armhole edge.

Shape left underarm

Next row *inc row:* (RS) Knit to last 3 sts, LLI, k1, p1, k1—1 st increased.

Next row: P1, k1, purl to end.

Rep these two rows 2 (2, 4, 5, 7, 8, 8, 7, 9, 10) more times—29 (30, 33, 35, 39, 41, 42, 43, 46, 48) sts.

Size 30" [76.5 cm]: skip to 'All sizes'
Sizes 33 to 57" [83.5 to 144.5 cm] only:

Next row: (RS) Knit to last 2 sts, p1, k1.

Next row: Cable CO – (2, 2, 2, 2, 3, 3, 2, 2, 3) sts, purl to end— – (32, 35, 37, 41, 44, 45, 45, 48, 51) sts.

Sizes 33 to 47½" [83.5 to 120.5 cm]: skip to 'All sizes'
Sizes 50¼ to 57" [128 to 144.5 cm] only:

Next row: (RS) Knit.

Next row: Cable CO – (–, –, –, –, –, –, 3, 3, 3) sts, purl to end— – (–, –, –, –, –, –, 48, 51, 54) sts.

All sizes
Piece should measure approx 7 (7¼, 7¾, 8¼, 8½, 8¾, 9, 9½, 9¾, 10)" [17.5 (18.5, 20, 20.5, 21.5, 22.5, 23, 24, 24.5, 25.5) cm] from shoulder seam to bottom, measured at armhole edge.

Join fronts to back

With RS facing, slip 60 (66, 72, 76, 84, 90, 94, 100, 106, 112) held back sts to left end of needle holding left front, then slip 29 (32, 35, 37, 41, 44, 45, 48, 51, 54) held right front sts to needle.

Left front: (RS) Knit across left front sts. Turn work to WS and cable CO 5 (5, 5, 7, 7, 7, 9, 9, 9, 11) sts.

Back: Turn work to RS. Slip last st cast on back to LH needle, k2tog with first back st, knit to end. Turn work to WS and cable CO 5 (5, 5, 7, 7, 7, 9, 9, 9, 11) sts.

Right front: Turn work to RS. Slip last st cast on back to LH needle, k2tog with first right front st, knit to end—126 (138, 150, 162, 178, 190, 200, 212, 224, 240) sts.

Next row: Purl.

BODICE

Markers are placed to indicate position of waist shaping darts. Front markers should be in line with, or just slightly to the outside of bust points.

Next row: (RS) K11 (12, 11, 14, 14, 15, 13, 14, 13, 14), **pm**, k39 (43, 48, 50, 56, 60, 65, 69, 74, 80), **pm**, k26 (28, 32, 34, 38, 40, 44, 46, 50, 52), **pm**, k39 (43, 48, 50, 56, 60, 65, 69, 74, 80), **pm**, knit to end.

Work even in stockinette stitch until bodice is approx ½ to 1" [1.5 to 2.5 cm] below apex of bust. End having worked a WS row.

Begin underbust decreases

Next row *dec row:* * Knit to marker, **sl m**, ssk, knit to 2 sts before next marker, k2tog, **sl m**; rep from * once more; work as established to end—4 sts decreased.

Next 3 rows: Work even in stockinette.

Rep these four rows two more times—114 (126, 138, 150, 166, 178, 188, 200, 212, 228) sts.

Work even until bodice is approx ¾ to 1" [2 to 2.5 cm] above waistline or narrowest part of torso. End having worked a WS row.

Begin hip increases

Next row *inc row:* * Knit to marker, **sl m**, RLI, knit to next marker, LLI, **sl m**; rep from * once more, knit to end—4 sts increased.

Next 3 rows: Work even in stockinette.

Rep these four rows 3 (3, 4, 4, 4, 4, 4, 4, 4, 4) more times—130 (142, 158, 170, 186, 198, 208, 220, 232, 248) sts.

Work even until piece measures 16¾ (17¼, 17¾, 18¼, 18¾, 19¼, 19¾, 20¼, 20¾, 21¼)" [42.5 (44, 45, 46.5, 47.5, 49, 50, 51.5, 52.5, 54) cm] from neck edge of shoulder to bottom, or desired length, less 4¾" [11.5 cm].

For Serif version, break yarn, then continue skirt following directions on page 51.

SKIRT

Row 1: (RS) K8 (8, 11, 11, 11, 14, 14, 14, 18, 18), place the next 16 (16, 20, 20, 20, 20, 20, 20, 20, 20) sts onto waste yarn, and using the cable cast-on, CO 16 (16, 20, 20, 20, 20, 20, 20, 20, 20) sts, knit to last 24 (24, 31, 31, 31, 34, 34, 34, 38, 38) sts, place the next 16 (16, 20, 20, 20, 20, 20, 20, 20, 20) sts onto waste yarn, cable CO 16 (16, 20, 20, 20, 20, 20, 20, 20, 20) sts, knit to end.

Row 2: Purl.

Work even until sweater measures 20¼ (20¾, 21¼, 21¾, 22¼, 22¾, 23¼, 23¾, 24¼, 24¾)" [51.5 (52.5, 54, 55, 56.5, 58, 59, 60.5, 61.5, 63) cm] from neck edge of shoulder to bottom, or desired length, less 1¼" [3 cm]. End having worked a WS row.

Hem

Change to US 7 [4.5 mm] circ.

Sizes 47½ to 57" [120.5 to 144.5 cm]: skip to 'All sizes'
Sizes 30 to 45¼" [76.5 to 114.5 cm] only:
Set-up Row 1: (RS) K3, p2tog, p1, [k2, p2] to last 8 sts, k2, p1, p2tog, k3—128 (140, 156, 168, 184, 196, –, –, –, –) sts.
Set-up Row 2: P3, k2, [p2, k2] to last 3 sts, p3.

All sizes
Row 1: (RS) K3, p2, [k2, p2] to last 3 sts, k3.
Row 2: P3, k2, [p2, k2] to last 3 sts, k3.
Rep these two rows 2 (2, 2, 2, 2, 3, 3, 3, 3) more times.
Bind off all stitches loosely in pattern.

SLEEVES

Note: Pick up stitches using US 7 [4.5 mm] circ, then transfer them to 16" [40 cm] long US 9 [5.5 mm] circ before beginning to work sleeve cap.

Place a removable stitch marker on front and back 1⅛ (1¼, 1¼, 1⅜, 1½, 1⅝, 1¾, 1⅞, 2, 2⅛)" [2.75 (3, 3.25, 3.5, 3.75, 4.25, 4.5, 4.75, 5, 5.25) cm] away from the shoulder seam. Place a third marker at the center of the underarm. The marker to right of shoulder seam is **M-one**, to left of shoulder is **M-two**, at underarm is **M-three**.

Begin at **M-one**. Working just inside the column of knit sts on the edge of armhole, pick up and knit 11 (11, 13, 15, 17, 19, 19, 20, 22, 22) sts between **M-one** and **M-two**, pick up and knit 21 (21, 22, 22, 23, 24, 25, 25, 26, 26) sts between **M-two** and the cast-on sts at underarm, **pm**, pick up and knit 1 st in each of the 2 (4, 4, 5, 5, 6, 7, 9, 9, 11) cast-on sts before **M-three**, place unique marker for beginning of round, pick up and knit 1 st in each of the remaining 2 (4, 4, 5, 5, 6, 7, 9, 9, 11) cast-on sts at underarm, **pm**, pick up and knit

21 (21, 22, 22, 23, 24, 25, 25, 26, 26) more sts, ending at **M-one**—57 (61, 65, 69, 73, 79, 83, 88, 92, 96) sts.

Remove **M-one**, **M-two** and **M-three**.

Shape upper cap

When working the short rows that shape the sleeve caps, the wraps are not picked up; they are left in place and the wrapped stitch is worked in the normal fashion.

Short Row 1: (RS) K11 (11, 13, 15, 17, 19, 19, 20, 22, 22), w&t; (WS) p11 (11, 13, 15, 17, 19, 19, 20, 22, 22), w&t.
Short Row 2: (RS) Knit to prev wrapped st, knit wrapped st, sl 1 wyif, shift yarn to back, w&t; (WS) purl to prev wrapped st, purl wrapped st, sl 1 wyib, bring yarn to front, w&t.
Rep Short Row 2 twice more.

Shape mid cap

Next short row: (RS) Knit to prev wrapped st, knit wrapped st, w&t; (WS) purl to prev wrapped st, purl wrapped st, w&t.

Rep this row, working back and forth to build the sleeve cap, until 5 sts remain before each of the side markers that separate the underarm sts from the sleeve cap.

Shape lower cap

Next short row: (RS) Knit to prev wrapped st, knit wrapped st, then wrap the next 2 sts together & turn; (WS) purl to prev wrapped st, purl wrapped st, then wrap the next 2 sts together & turn.

Next short row *dec row*: (RS) Knit to twin-wrapped sts, knit wrapped sts tog as one st, wrap 2 sts together & turn; (WS) purl to twin-wrapped sts, purl wrapped sts tog as one st, wrap 2 sts together & turn—2 sts decreased.

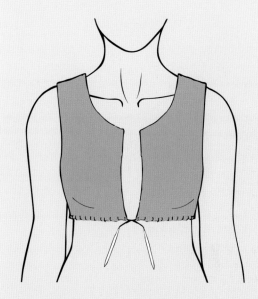

trying on as you go

As you knit, you'll be trying on your sweater and making decisions about when to begin bust and waist shaping based on how it actually fits. There's no need to slip your stitches to waste yarn to see if you've reached a particular milestone in the pattern. Just try your garment on right on the needles.

When knitting a cardigan, use circular needles of a sufficient length to go comfortably around your bust and/or hip circumference, and keep the work scrunched towards one end until you need to try it on. For a pullover, have a second needle of the same size handy, and use it to knit across half the stitches, giving yourself room to slip the garment on over your head.

Rep this row until 1 st remains before each side marker.

Next short row *dec row:* (RS) Knit to twin-wrapped sts, knit wrapped sts tog as one st, wrap next *single* st, remove marker & turn; (WS) purl to twin-wrapped sts, purl wrapped sts tog as one st, wrap next *single* st, remove marker & turn—53 (57, 61, 65, 69, 75, 79, 84, 88, 92) sts.

Last row *dec row:* (RS) Knit to prev wrapped st, k2tog-tbl with next st, k1 (3, 3, 4, 4, 5, 6, 8, 8, 10)—52 (56, 60, 64, 68, 74, 78, 83, 87, 91) sts.

Work sleeve in the round

Change to preferred needle style for small circumference knitting in the round when necessary.

Rnd 1 *dec rnd:* K1 (3, 3, 4, 4, 5, 6, 8, 8, 10), k2tog with remaining wrapped st, knit to end of round—51 (55, 59, 63, 67, 73, 77, 82, 86, 90) sts.

Next 2 rnds: Knit.

Next rnd *dec rnd:* K1, ssk, knit to last 3 sts, k2tog, k1—2 sts decreased.

For Serif version, continue sleeve following directions on page 52.

Work *dec rnd* every 7th (5th, 5th, 5th, 5th, 5th, 4th, 4th, 3rd, 3rd) rnd 3 (4, 4, 4, 4, 5, 5, 6, 6) more times, then every 14th (11th, 9th, 9th, 8th, 7th, 7th, 6th, 6th, 6th) rnd 5 (7, 8, 9, 10, 12, 12, 14, 14, 15) more times—33 (33, 33, 37, 37, 41, 41, 44, 44, 44) sts.

Sizes 50¼ to 57" [128 to 144.5 cm]: skip to 'All sizes'
Sizes 30 to 47½" [76.5 to 120.5 cm] only:

Next rnd *dec rnd:* Knit to last 3 sts, k2tog, k1—32 (32, 32, 36, 36, 40, 40, –, –, –) sts.

For Serif version, continue sleeve following directions on page 52.

All sizes

When decreases are complete, work even until sleeve measures 15 (15½, 15½, 16, 16, 16½, 16½, 17, 17, 17½)" [38 (39.5, 39.5, 40.5, 40.5, 42, 42, 43, 43, 44.5) cm] from underarm, or desired length, less 1½" [4 cm].

Cuff

Change to US 5 [3.75 mm] needles.

Rnd 1: [K2, p2] to end.

Rep this rnd 9 more times. Bind off all stitches loosely in pattern.

BANDS
Button band

The button band is worked in k2, p2 ribbing, edged with a crisp horizontal braid. The bottom stitch of the band is worked in garter stitch.

With RS facing, attach yarn at neck edge of left front. Using US 3 [3.25 mm] circ, pick up and knit 3 stitches for every 4 rows along edge of stockinette bodice, making sure to pick up a number of stitches that is divisible by four. Note the number of stitches picked up.

Change to US 5 [3.75 mm] circ.

Row 1: (WS) K1, purl to end.

Row 2: Knit.

Change to US 3 [3.25 mm] circ to work horizontal braid.

Row 3: Knit.

Row 4: Yo, k2tog-tbl, * sl st back to LH needle, yo, k2tog-tbl; rep from * to end.

Change to US 5 [3.75 mm] circ.

Row 5: K1, then purl-tbl to end.

Row 6: K3, [p2, k2] across row to last st, end k1.

Row 7: K1, then knit the knit sts and purl the purl sts.

Rep Rows 6 and 7 two more times, then work Row 5 once more. Bind off all stitches in pattern.

Buttonhole band

With RS facing, attach yarn at bottom edge of right front. Using US 3 [3.25 mm] circ, pick up and knit stitches as for button band, making sure to pick up the same number of stitches.

Change to US 5 [3.75 mm] circ. Work Rows 1–4 of button band instructions.

Change to US 5 [3.75 mm] circ. On the next row, markers are placed to indicate the lower edge of the five buttonholes to be worked on the band. A sixth buttonhole will be placed on the neckband. Adjust position of buttonholes as needed.

Row 5: (WS) P10 (10, 10, 10, 11, 11, 11, 12, 12, 12) through the back loop, **pm**, [p13 (13, 13, 13, 14, 14, 14, 15, 15, 15) through the back loop, **pm**] 4 times, purl-tbl to last st, k1-tbl.

Row 6: K1, then, mirroring pattern of button band, work in k2, p2 ribbing to last 3 sts, ending k3.

Row 7: Knit the knit sts and purl the purl sts to last st, end k1.

Next row *buttonhole bind-off row:* * Work in patt to marker, remove marker, bind off the next 2 sts; rep from * 4 more times, then work in patt to end.

Next row *buttonhole cast-on row:* * Work in patt to 1 st before gap, kfpb, then turn work and using the purled cast-on method, CO 2 sts. Turn work, slip last CO st to LH needle and purl it together with first st on needle; rep from * 4 more times, work in patt to end.

Next 3 rows: Work in patt.

Bind off all stitches loosely in pattern.

Neckband

With RS facing, attach yarn at neck edge of right front. Using US 3 [3.25 mm] circ, pick up and knit 10 sts across top of buttonhole band, 14 (15, 16, 17, 17, 17, 18, 18, 18, 19) sts between band and vertical edge of neckline, 26 (26, 27, 29, 30, 30, 32, 33, 33, 33) sts along right neck to shoulder, 36 (38, 38, 40, 42, 42, 44, 46, 46, 48) sts along back neck to left shoulder, 26 (26, 27, 29, 30, 30, 32, 33, 33, 33) sts along left neck, 14 (15, 16, 17, 17, 17, 18, 18, 18, 19) sts between vertical edge and band, and 10 more sts along top of button band—136 (140, 144, 152, 156, 156, 164, 168, 168, 172) sts.

Change to US 5 [3.75 mm] circ.

Row 1: (WS) K1, purl to last st, k1.

Row 2: Knit.

Change to US 3 [3.25 mm] circ to work horizontal braid.

Row 3: Knit.

Row 4: Yo, k2tog-tbl, * sl st back to LH needle, yo, k2tog-tbl; rep from * to end.

Change to US 5 [3.75 mm] circ.

Row 5: K1, purl-tbl to last st, k1.

Row 6: K3, [p2, k2] across row to last st, end k1.

Row 7: K1, then knit the knit sts and purl the purl sts across row to last st, k1.

Next row *buttonhole bind-off row:* K3, bind off the next 2 sts, then work in ribbing patt to last st, k1.

Next row *buttonhole cast-on row:* K1, work in patt to 1 st before gap, kfpb, then turn work and using the purled cast-on method, CO 2 sts. Turn work, slip last CO st to LH needle and purl it together with first st on needle, p2, k1.

Next 3 rows: Work in established ribbing patt, keeping edge sts in garter stitch.

Bind off all stitches in pattern.

POCKETS

Pocket edging

With RS facing, using US 3 [3.25 mm] circ, pick up and knit 1 st to right of cast-on pocket stitches, 1 stitch in each cast-on stitch, and 1 stitch after pocket sts—18 (18, 22, 22, 22, 22, 22, 22, 22, 22) sts.

Set-up row *inc row:* (WS) Kfb, knit to last st, kfb—20 (20, 24, 24, 24, 24, 24, 24, 24, 24) sts.

Row 1: Yo, k2tog-tbl, * sl st back to LH needle, yo, k2tog-tbl; rep from * to end.

Change to US 5 [3.75 mm] circ.

Row 2: P1, purl-tbl to last st.

Row 3: K3, [p2, k2] to last 3 sts, k3.

Row 4: P3, k2, [p2, k2] to last 3 sts, p3.

Rep Rows 3 and 4 two more times, then bind off all stitches in pattern.

Pocket linings

Return 16 (16, 20, 20, 20, 20, 20, 20, 20, 20) held pocket stitches to US 9 [5.5 mm] circ. With fingering-weight yarn and long tail cast-on, CO 2 sts to empty end of needle.

Set-up Row 1: (RS) Knit across pocket stitches—18 (18, 22, 22, 22, 22, 22, 22, 22, 22) sts.

Set-up Row 2: Cable CO 2 sts, purl to end—20 (20, 24, 24, 24, 24, 24, 24, 24, 24) sts.

Work even in stockinette until pocket lining is approx 1" [2.5 cm] shorter than body length. End having worked a RS row.

Change to US 3 [3.25 mm] circ.

Next row *turning row:* (WS) Yo, k2tog-tbl, * sl st back to LH needle, yo, k2tog-tbl; rep from * to end.

Change to US 9 [5.5 mm] circ.

Next row: K1, knit-tbl to end.

Work even in stockinette until the same number of rows have been worked on either side of the turning ridge. End having worked a RS row.

Break yarn, leaving a 24" [60 cm] tail. Place pocket stitches on waste yarn.

FINISHING

Whip-stitch sides of pocket closed, then press pocket flat using a steam iron and damp pressing cloth. Take care to press pocket lining only, not garment.

Using tail yarn, sew lining to selvedge edge of pocket opening, along the same line where sts were picked up for edging. Stitch sides of pocket edgings to sweater body. Weave in all ends. Block sweater to measurements. Sew on buttons.

serif *Sport*

A modern riff on Sans Serif, this version is designed to show how a few simple changes can utterly transform a garment. The design uses two different weights of yarn, Lark for the main body of the sweater, and Chickadee for the skirt, cuffs and bands. The two fabrics have a similar weight and hand, and allow for a lot of fun color-blocking possibilities. Measurements, gauge, and needle sizes are the same as for Sans Serif, except where noted.

Materials

Main yarn
Lark by Quince & Co.
(100% American wool; 134 yd [123 m] / 50 g)

• 5 (6, 6, 6, 7, 7, 8, 9, 10, 10) skeins Sedum (142)

Contrast yarn
Chickadee by Quince & Co. *Sport*
(100% American wool; 181 yd [166 m] / 50 g)

• 3 (4, 4, 4, 4, 4, 4, 5, 5, 5) skeins Twig (119)

Additional needles

Body
• US 5 [3.75 mm] circ, 32" [80 cm] long or longer

Bands
• US 1 [2.25 mm] circ, 24" [60 cm] long,
  for picking up stitches
Or size to obtain gauge

Notions

• Waste yarn of similar gauge and contrasting color
• Stitch markers, both removable and fixed ring,
  including one unique
• 7 buttons, ⅞" [23 mm] in diameter
• Yarn needle

Gauge for Chickadee

22 sts and 52 rows = 4" [10 cm] in garter stitch, worked flat, on US 5 [3.75 mm] needles, after blocking.

~

Follow instructions for Sans Serif through 'Hip increases', then continue skirt as follows:

GARTER STITCH SKIRT

To adjust for the difference in gauge between the stockinette fabric of the body and the garter fabric of the skirt, yarnover increases are made. On the following row, the yarnovers are worked through the back loop to close them up. Take care to keep yarnovers as small as possible.

Change to US 5 [3.75 mm] circ. With RS facing, attach contrast yarn.

Pocket set-up

Before beginning set-up rows, mark position of pockets by placing 2 locking stitch markers 8 (8, 11, 11, 11, 14, 14, 14, 18, 18) sts from each end of needle, and 2 more locking markers 25 (28, 31, 31, 31, 34, 36, 36, 40, 40) sts from each end of needle.

Set-up Row 1: (RS) K1, [k3, yo] 2 (2, 3, 3, 3, 4, 4, 4, 5, 5) times, knit to marker, **sl m**, k17 (20, 20, 20, 20, 20, 22, 22, 22, 22), **sl m**, k0 (0, 1, 1, 3, 3, 3, 3, 2, 4), [k3, yo] 26 (28, 30, 34, 38, 40, 42, 46, 48, 52) times, knit to marker, **sl m**, k17 (20, 20, 20, 20, 20, 22, 22, 22, 22), **sl m**, k1, [k3, yo] 2 (2, 3, 3, 3, 4, 4, 4, 5, 5) times, knit to end—30 (32, 36, 40, 44, 48, 50, 54, 58, 62) sts increased, 160 (174, 194, 210, 230, 246, 258, 274, 290, 310) sts total.

Set-up Row 2: * Knit to marker, working all yos through the back loop to twist, remove markers as you come to them and place the next 17 (20, 20, 20, 20, 20, 22, 22, 22, 22) sts onto waste yarn, then, using the backwards loop method, CO 21 (25, 25, 25, 25, 25, 27, 27, 27, 27) sts; rep from * once more, knit to end working yos tbl—8 (10, 10, 10, 10, 10, 10, 10, 10, 10) sts increased, 168 (184, 204, 220, 240, 256, 268, 284, 300, 320) sts total.

No-pocket set-up

Set-up Row 1: (RS) [K2, yo] twice, [k4, yo, k3, yo] 17 (19, 21, 23, 25, 27, 28, 30, 32, 34) times, [k2, yo] twice, knit to end—168 (184, 204, 220, 240, 256, 268, 284, 300, 320) sts.

Set-up Row 2: Knit, working all yos through the back loop to twist.

Work skirt

Work even in garter stitch, knitting all rows, for 60 rows (30 garter ridges), or until skirt reaches desired length.

Bind off all stitches loosely.

Pocket linings

Return 17 (20, 20, 20, 20, 20, 22, 22, 22, 22) held pocket stitches to US 5 [3.75 mm] circ. Using contrast yarn and the long tail cast-on, CO 2 sts to empty end of needle.

Set-up Row 1: (RS) Knit across pocket stitches—19 (22, 22, 22, 22, 22, 24, 24, 24, 24) sts.

Set-up Row 2: Backwards loop CO 2 sts, purl to end—21 (24, 24, 24, 24, 24, 26, 26, 26, 26) sts.

Change to US 9 [5.5 mm] circ.

Work even in stockinette until pocket lining is approx 1" [2.5 cm] shorter than garter skirt. Bind off all sts.

SLEEVES

Follow sleeve instructions for Sans Serif through the first three rounds of 'Work sleeve in the round', then continue sleeve as follows:

Next rnd *dec rnd:* K1, ssk, knit to last 3 sts, k2tog, k1—2 sts decreased.

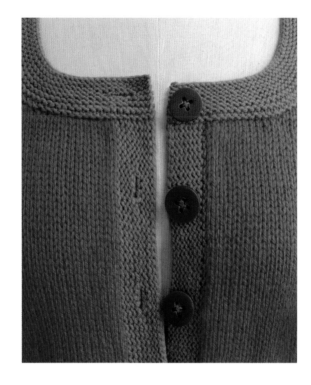

Work *dec rnd* every 21st (13th, 11th, 10th, 9th, 7th, 7th, 6th, 6th, 5th) rnd 3 (4, 5, 6, 7, 9, 10, 12, 13, 14) more times—43 (45, 47, 49, 51, 53, 55, 56, 58, 60) sts.

Work even until sleeve measures approx 10½ (11, 11, 11½, 11½, 12, 12, 12½, 12½, 13)" [26.5 (28, 28, 29, 29, 30.5, 30.5, 32, 32, 33) cm] from underarm, or desired length, less 6" [15 cm].

Break yarn.

Cuffs

The sleeve cuffs are worked flat in garter stitch, then seamed. If you prefer to work them in the round, omit the cast-on stitch at the end of the first set-up row, and purl every other round.

Change to US 5 [3.75 mm] circ. Attach contrast yarn.

Set-up Row 1: (RS) K0 (1, 1, 0, 1, 1, 2, 1, 2, 2), [k3, yo] 12 (12, 13, 14, 14, 15, 15, 16, 16, 17) times, knit to end, then backwards loop CO 1 more st—53 (55, 58, 61, 63, 66, 68, 71, 73, 76) sts.

Set-up Row 2: Knit, working all yos through the back loop to twist.

Row 1: Knit.

Rep this row 7 more times.

Next row *dec row:* (RS) K1, ssk, knit to last 4 sts, k2tog, k2—2 sts decreased.

Work *dec row* every 10th (10th, 10th, 8th, 8th, 8th, 8th, 8th, 8th, 8th) row 6 (6, 6, 7, 7, 7, 7, 7, 7, 7) more times—39 (41, 44, 45, 47, 50, 52, 55, 57, 60) sts.

Work even until a total of 78 rows (39 garter ridges) have been worked, or until sleeve reaches desired length.

Bind off all stitches loosely, leaving a 16" [40 cm] long tail. Seam cuff using tail, instructions page 53 .

BANDS
Button band

With RS facing, attach contrast yarn at neck edge of left front. Using US 1 [2.25 mm] circ, pick up and knit 4 stitches for every 5 rows along edge of stockinette bodice. Continue picking up along edge of garter skirt, inserting needle into the furrow between the garter ridges, at a rate of 4 stitches for every 5 garter ridges. Make a note of the number of stitches picked up.

Change to US 3 [3.25 mm] circ.

Row 1: (WS) Knit.

Rep this row 14 more times. End having worked a WS row. Bind off all stitches loosely.

Buttonhole band

With RS facing, attach contrast yarn at bottom edge of right front. Using US 1 [2.25 mm] circ, pick up and knit stitches as for button band, making sure to pick up the same number of stitches.

On the next row, markers are placed to indicate the lower edges of the six buttonholes to be worked on the band. A seventh buttonhole will be placed on the neckband. Adjust position of buttonholes as needed.

Change to US 3 [3.25 mm] circ.

Set-up row: (WS) K10 (10, 10, 11, 11, 11, 11, 11, 12, 12), **pm**, [k13 (13, 13, 14, 14, 14, 14, 14, 15, 15), **pm**] 5 times, knit to end.

Row 1: Knit.

Rep this row five more times, ending with a WS row.

Next row: * Knit to marker, remove marker, bind off the next 3 sts; rep from * 5 more times, then knit to end.

Next row: * Knit to 1 st before gap, kfb, then turn work and using the purled cast-on method, CO 3 sts. Turn work, slip last CO st to LH needle and knit it together with first st on needle; rep from * 5 more times, then knit to end.

Next 6 rows: Knit, ending with a WS row.

Bind off all stitches loosely, but do not break yarn—1 st remains.

Neckband

Slip remaining stitch to US 1 [2.25 mm] circ.

Pick-up row: (RS) Counting remaining st as first st, pick up and knit 6 more sts across top of buttonhole band, 14 (15, 15, 16, 17, 17, 17, 18, 18, 19) sts between band and vertical edge of right neckline, 26 (26, 27, 29, 29, 30, 32, 32, 33, 33) sts along right neck to shoulder, 36 (38, 38, 40, 42, 42, 44, 46, 46, 48) sts along back neck to left

shoulder, 26 (26, 27, 29, 29, 30, 32, 32, 33, 33) sts along left neck, 14 (15, 15, 16, 17, 17, 17, 18, 18, 19) sts between vertical edge and band, and 7 more sts along top of button band—130 (134, 136, 144, 148, 150, 156, 160, 162, 166) sts.

Change to US 5 [3.75 mm] circ.

Rows 1–6: Knit.

Change to US 3 [3.25 mm] circ.

Row 7: (WS) Knit.

Row 8: K4, bind off the next 3 sts, knit to end.

Row 9: Knit to 1 st before gap, work buttonhole CO as for buttonhole band, knit to end.

Next 6 rows: Knit, ending with a WS row.

Bind off all stitches firmly.

FINISHING

Weave in all ends. Block sweater to measurements. Whip-stitch pocket linings to skirt. Sew on buttons.

seaming garter stitch

In garter stitch fabric, each ridge is composed of two sets of purl bumps. The top-most ones turn downwards like umbrellas, and the bottom ones turn upwards like smiles. To seam garter fabric, you'll join a column of umbrellas on one edge to a column of smiles on the other.

Arrange the work so that the edges to be seamed are side-by-side, right sides facing. Thread the existing tail onto a yarn needle. Pass it under both legs of the first bound-off stitch on the opposite edge, then bring it back through the center of the stitch that it comes from, joining the two edges of the work.

Select a column of smiles on one edge, and umbrellas on the other. For a more secure seam, make sure that one of the columns is right on the edge of the fabric, and the other is one stitch in from the edge.

Begin by inserting the needle, from bottom to top, into the first smile. Pull the yarn through, then insert the needle into the corresponding umbrella on the other side, going in from the bottom and out the top.

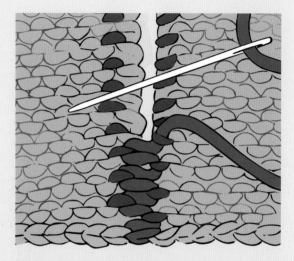

Continue in this fashion, weaving the yarn back and forth from smile to umbrella, as you work your way up the seam. Pull the yarn gently to snug up the stitches, matching the tension of the joined pieces.

For more information, watch this video tutorial: https://vimeo.com/128883334

underwood

With its textured herringbone panels at the neckline, cuffs and hem, Underwood is a modern take on the fisherman's gansey. A square neckline frames the face. The slipped-stitch ribs of the herringbone pattern are carried through the design for accents at the cuffs and side panels. And to keep the line clean, bust and waist shaping are worked invisibly into the ribbed side panels.

Finished measurements

Shoulder width: 12¼ (13, 13¼, 13¾, 14¼, 15, 16¼, 17, 17¼, 18)" [31 (33, 33.5, 34.5, 36.5, 38.5, 41, 43, 44, 45.5) cm]

Bust circumference: 30¼ (32½, 36¼, 38½, 42, 45¼, 48, 51, 53½, 57)" [76.5 (82.5, 92, 97.5, 106.5, 115, 122, 129.5, 136, 145) cm]

Sample shown in 13¾" [34.5 cm] shoulder, 38½" [97.5 cm] bust size.

Suggested ease at bust: -1 to +1" [-2.5 to +2.5 cm]

Materials
Yarn

Sport

Chickadee by Quince & Co.
(100% American wool; 181 yd [166 m] / 50 g)

• 7 (8, 8, 8, 9, 9, 10, 11, 12, 12) skeins Nasturtium (136)

Needles

Body
• US 6 [4 mm] circ, 24" [60 cm] long or longer

Sleeves
• US 6 [4 mm] circ, 16" [40 cm] long
• US 6 [4 mm] needles of preferred style for
  working small circumferences in the round

Or size to obtain gauge

Optional
• Extra US 6 [4 mm] circ to facilitate trying on garment
• US 2 [2.75 mm] circ for picking up stitches

Notions
• Waste yarn of a similar weight and contrasting color
• Stitch markers, both removable and fixed ring,
  including one unique for beginning of round
• Yarn needle

Gauge

22 sts and 34 rows/rnds = 4" [10 cm] in stockinette stitch on US 6 [4 mm] needles, after blocking.

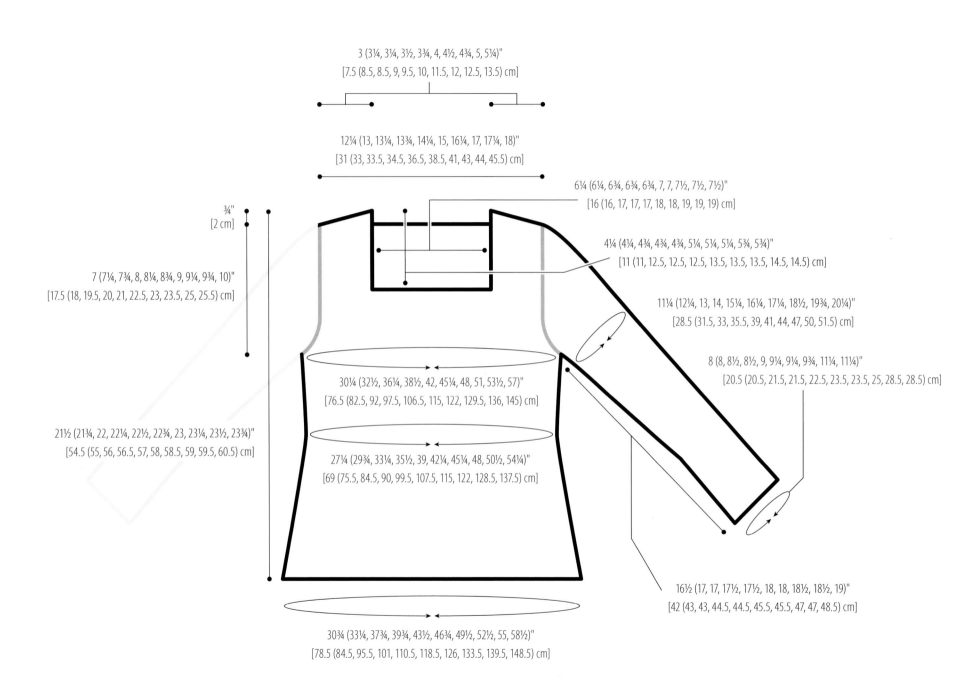

3 (3¼, 3¼, 3½, 3¾, 4, 4½, 4¾, 5, 5¼)"
[7.5 (8.5, 8.5, 9, 9.5, 10, 11.5, 12, 12.5, 13.5) cm]

12¼ (13, 13¼, 13¾, 14¼, 15, 16¼, 17, 17¼, 18)"
[31 (33, 33.5, 34.5, 36.5, 38.5, 41, 43, 44, 45.5) cm]

6¼ (6¼, 6¾, 6¾, 6¾, 7, 7, 7½, 7½, 7½)"
[16 (16, 17, 17, 17, 18, 18, 19, 19, 19) cm]

¾"
[2 cm]

4¼ (4¼, 4¾, 4¾, 4¾, 5¼, 5¼, 5¼, 5¾, 5¾)"
[11 (11, 12.5, 12.5, 12.5, 13.5, 13.5, 13.5, 14.5, 14.5) cm]

7 (7¼, 7¾, 8, 8¼, 8¾, 9, 9¼, 9¾, 10)"
[17.5 (18, 19.5, 20, 21, 22.5, 23, 23.5, 25, 25.5) cm]

11¼ (12¼, 13, 14, 15¼, 16¼, 17¼, 18½, 19¾, 20¼)"
[28.5 (31.5, 33, 35.5, 39, 41, 44, 47, 50, 51.5) cm]

30¼ (32½, 36¼, 38½, 42, 45¼, 48, 51, 53½, 57)"
[76.5 (82.5, 92, 97.5, 106.5, 115, 122, 129.5, 136, 145) cm]

8 (8, 8½, 8½, 9, 9¼, 9¼, 9¾, 11¼, 11¼)"
[20.5 (20.5, 21.5, 21.5, 22.5, 23.5, 23.5, 25, 28.5, 28.5) cm]

21½ (21¾, 22, 22¼, 22½, 22¾, 23, 23¼, 23½, 23¾)"
[54.5 (55, 56, 56.5, 57, 58, 58.5, 59, 59.5, 60.5) cm]

27¼ (29¾, 33¼, 35½, 39, 42¼, 45¼, 48, 50½, 54¼)"
[69 (75.5, 84.5, 90, 99.5, 107.5, 115, 122, 128.5, 137.5) cm]

16½ (17, 17, 17½, 17½, 18, 18, 18½, 18½, 19)"
[42 (43, 43, 44.5, 44.5, 45.5, 45.5, 47, 47, 48.5) cm]

30¾ (33¼, 37¾, 39¾, 43½, 46¾, 49½, 52½, 55, 58½)"
[78.5 (84.5, 95.5, 101, 110.5, 118.5, 126, 133.5, 139.5, 148.5) cm]

BACK (begin at right shoulder)

With US 6 [4 mm] circ and the long-tail cast-on, loosely CO 17 (19, 19, 20, 22, 23, 26, 27, 28, 30) sts.

Set-up row: (WS) P1, k1, purl to last 5 sts, k5.

Shape right shoulder

Short Row 1: (RS) K4, p1, k1 (1, 1, 1, 1, 1, 1, 2, 2, 2), w&t; (WS) p1 (1, 1, 1, 1, 1, 1, 2, 2, 2), k5.

Short Row 2: (RS) K4, p1, knit to wrapped st, pick up wrap, k3 (4, 4, 4, 4, 5, 6, 6, 6, 7), w&t; (WS) purl to last 5 sts, k5.

Short Row 3: Rep Short Row 2.

Row 4: K4, p1, knit to last 2 sts, picking up wrap, p1, k1.

Row 5: P1, k1, purl to last 5 sts, k5.

Break yarn and slip stitches onto waste yarn.

Left shoulder

With US 6 [4 mm] circ and the long-tail cast-on, loosely CO 17 (19, 19, 20, 22, 23, 26, 27, 28, 30) sts.

Set-up row: (WS) K5, purl to last 2 sts, k1, p1.

Row 1: K1, p1, knit to last 5 sts, p1, k4.

Shape left shoulder

Short Row 1: (WS) K5, p1 (1, 1, 1, 1, 1, 1, 2, 2, 2), w&t; (RS) k1 (1, 1, 1, 1, 1, 1, 2, 2, 2), p1, k4.

Short Row 2: (WS) K5, purl to wrapped st, pick up wrap, p3 (4, 4, 4, 4, 5, 6, 6, 6, 7), w&t; (RS) knit to last 5 sts, p1, k4.

Short Row 3: Rep Short Row 2.

Row 4: K5, purl to last 2 sts, picking up wrap, k1, p1. Tie a yarn marker around the last stitch of Row 4.

Join shoulders

With RS facing, slip 17 (19, 19, 20, 22, 23, 26, 27, 28, 30) held right shoulder sts to left end of needle holding left shoulder sts.

Left shoulder: (RS) K1, p1, knit to last 5 sts, **pm**, p1, [k1-tbl, p1] twice.

Back neck: Turn work to WS and cable CO 36 (36, 38, 38, 38, 40, 40, 42, 42, 42) sts.

Right shoulder: Turn work to RS. Slip last st cast on back to LH needle, p2tog with first right shoulder st, [k1-tbl, p1] twice, **pm**, knit to last 2 sts, p1, k1—69 (73, 75, 77, 81, 85, 91, 95, 97, 101) sts.

Work twisted rib edging

Set-up row: (WS) P1, k1, purl to marker, **sl m**, k1, [p1-tbl, k1] to marker, **sl m**, purl to last 2 sts, k1, p1.

Row 1: K1, p1, knit to marker, **sl m**, p1, [k1-tbl, p1] to next marker, **sl m**, knit to last 2 sts, p1, k1.

Row 2: P1, k1, purl to marker, **sl m**, k1, [p1-tbl, k1] to next marker, **sl m**, purl to last 2 sts, k1, p1.

Row 3: K1, p1, knit to marker, **sl m**, p1, k1-tbl, [k1, k1-tbl] to 1 st before marker, p1, **sl m**, knit to last 2 sts, p1, k1.

Row 4: P1, k1, purl to marker, **sl m**, knit to marker, **sl m**, purl to last 2 sts, k1, p1.

Continue back

Remove neckline markers as you come to them.

Row 1: (RS) K1, p1, knit to last 2 sts, p1, k1.

Row 2: P1, k1, purl to last 2 sts, k1, p1.

Rep Rows 1 and 2 until 46 (46, 42, 42, 42, 40, 42, 44, 44, 40) rows have been worked from yarn marker. Piece should measure approx 5¾ (5¾, 5¼, 5¼, 5¼, 5, 5¼, 5½, 5½, 5)" [14.5 (14.5, 13.5, 13.5, 13.5, 13, 13.5, 14, 14, 13) cm] from cast-on to bottom, measured at armhole edge.

Shape underarms

Next row *inc row:* (RS) K1, p1, k1, RLI, knit to last 3 sts, LLI, k1, p1, k1—2 sts increased.

Next row: P1, k1, purl to last 2 sts, k1, p1.

Rep these two rows 4 (4, 8, 9, 11, 14, 14, 13, 15, 18) more times—79 (83, 93, 97, 105, 115, 121, 123, 129, 139) sts.

Size 30¼" [76.5 cm]: skip to 'All sizes'
Sizes 32½ to 57" [82.5 to 145 cm] only:

Next row: (RS) Cable CO – (2, 2, 2, 3, 3, 3, 3, 3, 3) sts, knit to end— – (85, 95, 99, 108, 118, 124, 126, 132, 142) sts.

Next row: Cable CO – (2, 2, 2, 3, 3, 3, 3, 3, 3) sts, purl to end— – (87, 97, 101, 111, 121, 127, 129, 135, 145) sts.

Sizes 32½ to 48" [82.5 to 122 cm]: skip to 'All sizes'
Sizes 51 to 57" [129.5 to 145 cm] only:

Next row: (RS) Cable CO – (–, –, –, –, –, –, 3, 3, 3) sts, knit to end— – (–, –, –, –, –, –, 132, 138, 148) sts.

Next row: Cable CO – (–, –, –, –, –, –, 3, 3, 3) sts, purl to end— – (–, –, –, –, –, –, 135, 141, 151) sts.

All sizes

Piece should measure approx 7 (7¼, 7¾, 8, 8¼, 8¾, 9, 9¼, 9¾, 10)" [17.5 (18, 19.5, 20, 20.5, 22, 22.5, 23, 24.5, 25) cm] from cast-on to bottom, measured at armhole edge.

Break yarn and slip stitches onto waste yarn.

FRONT
Pick up for left front shoulder

With RS facing, attach yarn at neck edge of back left shoulder. With US 6 [4 mm] needle, pick up and knit 16 (18, 18, 19, 21, 22, 25, 26, 27, 29) stitches along cast-on edge, making sure to insert needle under both legs of each cast-on stitch.

Set-up row *inc row:* (WS) Pfkb, purl to last 5 sts, k5—17 (19, 19, 20, 22, 23, 26, 27, 28, 30) sts.

Work shoulder shaping, following instructions for back right shoulder. When shaping is complete, tie a yarn marker to the last stitch of the row just worked, then work even, as established, for 28 (28, 32, 32, 32, 36, 36, 36, 40, 40) rows, ending with a WS row.

Break yarn and slip stitches onto waste yarn.

Pick up for right front shoulder

With RS of back facing, attach yarn at armhole edge of back right shoulder. With US 6 [4 mm] needle, pick up and knit 16 (18, 18, 19, 21, 22, 25, 26, 27, 29) stitches, beginning at armhole edge.

Set-up row *inc row:* (WS) K5, purl to last 2 sts, pfkb, p1—17 (19, 19, 20, 22, 23, 26, 27, 28, 30) sts.

Row 1: K1, p1, knit to last 5 sts, p1, k4.

Work shoulder shaping, following instructions for back left shoulder. When shaping is complete, tie a yarn marker to the last stitch of the row just worked, then work even, as established, for 28 (28, 32, 32, 32, 36, 36, 36, 40, 40) rows, ending with a WS row.

Join shoulders

Following instructions for back neckline, join shoulder pieces to form front neckline—69 (73, 75, 77, 81, 85, 91, 95, 97, 101) sts.

Front neckline ribbing

Work twisted rib edging as for back neckline.

Front panel and underarm shaping

A herringbone-stitch panel will be worked at the neckline (see page 62 for written instructions and page 63 for chart). Underarm shaping will begin before the front panel is complete. Read ahead to anticipate.

Next row: (RS) K1, p1, knit to marker, **sl m**, p1, then beginning where indicated for your size, work Row 1 of front panel, p1, **sl m**, knit to last 2 sts, p1, k1.

Next 3 rows: Continue as established, working the first and last stitch between markers in reverse stockinette, and working the subsequent rows of herringbone pattern over the remaining 43 (43, 45, 45, 45, 47, 47, 49, 49, 49) stitches between markers. Maintain purled 'gutter' at each edge of piece.

Work all rows of front panel four times, then work Rows 1–3 once more. Once panel is complete, remove markers and work all sts between purled 'gutters' in stockinette.

At the same time, once 46 (46, 42, 42, 42, 40, 42, 44, 44, 40) rows have been worked from yarn marker, and piece measures approx 5¾ (5¾, 5¼, 5¼, 5¼, 5, 5¼, 5½, 5½, 5)" [14.5 (14.5, 13.5, 13.5, 13.5, 13, 13.5, 14, 14, 13) cm] from shoulder seam to bottom at armhole edge, begin underarm shaping.

Work underarm increases, following instructions for back—79 (87, 97, 101, 111, 121, 127, 135, 141, 151) sts.

Join front to back

With RS facing, slip 79 (87, 97, 101, 111, 121, 127, 135, 141, 151) held back sts to left end of needle holding front.

Front and left underarm: (RS) Knit across front sts. Turn work to WS and cable CO 3 (3, 3, 4, 4, 4, 5, 5, 6, 6) sts, **pm**, cable CO 4 (4, 4, 5, 5, 5, 6, 6, 7, 7) more sts.

Back and right underarm: Turn work to RS. Slip last st cast on back to LH needle, k2tog with first back st, knit across back sts. Turn work to WS and cable CO 3 (3, 3, 4, 4, 4, 5, 5, 6, 6) sts, place unique marker for beginning of round, cable CO 4 (4, 4, 5, 5, 5, 6, 6, 7, 7) more sts.

Join-up: Turn work to RS. Slip last st cast on back to LH needle, k2tog with first front st to join in round —170 (186, 206, 218, 238, 258, 274, 290, 306, 326) sts.

Set-up rnd: K0 (3, 3, 2, 2, 5, 4, 4, 6, 6), k1-tbl, **pm**, knit to 5 (8, 8, 8, 8, 11, 11, 11, 14, 14) sts before underarm marker, **pm**, k1-tbl, k4 (7, 7, 7, 7, 10, 10, 10, 13, 13), **sl m**, k4 (7, 7, 7, 7, 10, 10, 10, 13, 13), k1-tbl, **pm**, knit to 5 (8, 8, 8, 8, 11, 11, 11, 14, 14) sts before marker, **pm**, k1-tbl, k4 (7, 7, 7, 7, 10, 10, 10, 13, 13).

BODICE

Begin slip-stitch side panels

There are now 10 (16, 16, 16, 16, 22, 22, 22, 28, 28) sts between the outermost markers under each arm. Panels of slipped stitches will be worked over these stitches from this point to the ribbing at hem.

Decreases and increases for waist shaping will be made invisibly at the edges of these panels.

Rnd 1 *slip rnd:* * K1, sl 1, [k2, sl 1] to marker, **sl m**, knit to next marker, **sl m**, [sl 1, k2] to 2 sts before marker, sl 1, k1, **sl m**; rep from * to end.

Rnd 2 *knit-tbl rnd:* * K1, k1-tbl, [k2, k1-tbl] to marker, **sl m**, knit to next marker, **sl m**, [k1-tbl, k2] to 2 sts before marker, k1-tbl, k1, **sl m**; rep from * to end.

Rep Rnds 1 and 2 until bodice is approx ½ to 1" [1.5 to 2.5 cm] below apex of bust. End having worked a knit-tbl rnd. On the final round, shift the four markers that define the side panels one stitch closer to the center underarm markers.

Begin underbust decreases

Next rnd *dec set-up rnd:* Continue slip-stitch pattern, working in est patts to 1 st before *second* marker, sl 1-tbl, **sl m**, work in est patts to *fifth* marker, sl 1-tbl, **sl m**, work in patt to end.

Next rnd *dec rnd:* * Work in est patts to marker, **sl m**, k2tog-tbl, knit to 2 sts before marker, k2tog, **sl m**, work in est patts to marker, **sl m**; rep from * to end—4 sts decreased.

Next 2 rnds: Work *slip* and *knit-tbl rnds*.

Rep these four rnds three more times—154 (170, 190, 202, 222, 242, 258, 274, 290, 310) sts.

Once underbust decreases are complete, shift markers back to the outsides of the slip-stitch side panels. Work even in est patts until bodice is approx ¾ to 1" [2 to 2.5 cm] above waistline or narrowest part of torso. End having worked a slip rnd.

Begin hip increases

Next rnd *inc rnd:* * Work in est patts to marker, **sl m**, RLI, knit to 1 st before next marker, LLI, **sl m**, work in est patts to marker; rep from * to end—4 sts increased.

Next 3 rnds: Work even in est patts.

Rep these four rnds 4 (4, 5, 5, 5, 5, 5, 5, 5) more times—174 (190, 214, 226, 246, 266, 282, 298, 314, 334) sts.

Work even until sweater measures 17¾ (18, 18¼, 18½, 18¾, 19, 19¼, 19½, 19¾, 20)" [45 (45.5, 46.5, 47, 47.5, 48.5, 49, 49.5, 50, 51) cm] from neck edge of shoulder to bottom, or desired length, less 3¾" [9.5 cm]. End having worked a *knit-tbl* rnd.

Hem

Beginning where indicated for your size, work hem pattern (see page 62 for written instructions and page 63 for chart) over the 77 (79, 91, 97, 107, 111, 119, 127, 129, 139) sts between markers on front and back as follows:

Rnd 1: * Work slip-stitch panel to marker, **sl m**, work Rnd 1 of hem pattern to marker, **sl m**, work slip-stitch panel to marker, **sl m**; rep from * to end.

Rnds 2–4: Continue as established, working slip-stitch panels at the sides, and subsequent rnds of her-ringbone pattern on front and back.

Rep these four rnds seven more times. Slip-stitch panels are complete.

Twisted ribbing

Rnd 1: Purl.

Rnd 2: Knit.

Rnds 3–5: [K1-tbl, p1] to end.

Bind off all stitches in pattern.

SLEEVES

Note: Pick up stitches using smaller gauge needle, then transfer them to 16" [40 cm] long US 6 [4 mm] circ before beginning to work sleeve cap.

Place a removable stitch marker on front and back 1⅛ (1¼, 1¼, 1⅜, 1½, 1⅝, 1¾, 1⅞, 2, 2⅛)" [2.75 (3, 3.25, 3.5, 3.75, 4.25, 4.5, 4.75, 5, 5.25) cm] away from the shoulder seam. Place a third marker at the center of the under-arm. The marker to right of shoulder seam is **M-one**, to left of shoulder is **M-two**, at underarm is **M-three**.

Begin at **M-one**. Working just inside the column of knit sts on the edge of armhole, pick up and knit 16 (16, 17, 19, 22, 23, 25, 28, 30, 30) sts between **M-one** and **M-two**, pick up and knit 25 (26, 27, 28, 29, 31, 32, 31, 32, 34) sts between **M-two** and the cast-on sts at underarm, **pm**, pick up and knit 1 st in each of the 3 (5, 5, 6, 7, 7, 8, 11, 12, 12) cast-on sts before **M-three**, place unique marker for beginning of round, pick up and knit 1 st in each of the remaining 3 (5, 5, 6, 7, 7, 8, 11, 12, 12) cast-on sts at underarm, **pm**, pick up and knit 25 (26, 27, 28, 29, 31, 32, 31, 32, 34) more sts, ending at **M-one**—72 (78, 81, 87, 94, 99, 105, 112, 118, 122) sts.

Remove **M-one**, **M-two** and **M-three**.

Shape upper cap

When working the short rows that shape the sleeve caps, the wraps are not picked up; they are left in place and the wrapped stitch is worked in the normal fashion.

Short Row 1: (RS) K16 (16, 17, 19, 22, 23, 25, 28, 30, 30), w&t; (WS) p16 (16, 17, 19, 22, 23, 25, 28, 30, 30), w&t.

Short Row 2: (RS) Knit to prev wrapped st, knit wrapped st, sl 1 wyif, shift yarn to back, w&t; (WS) purl to prev wrapped st, purl wrapped st, sl 1 wyib, bring yarn to front, w&t.

Rep Short Row 2 twice more.

Shape mid cap

Next short row: (RS) Knit to prev wrapped st, knit wrapped st, w&t; (WS) purl to prev wrapped st, purl wrapped st, w&t.

Rep this row, working back and forth to build the sleeve cap, until 7 sts remain before each of the side markers that separate the underarm sts from the sleeve cap.

Shape lower cap

Next short row: (RS) Knit to prev wrapped st, knit wrapped st, then wrap the next 2 sts together & turn; (WS) purl to prev wrapped st, purl wrapped st, then wrap the next 2 sts together & turn.

Next short row *dec row:* (RS) Knit to twin-wrapped sts, knit wrapped sts tog as one st, wrap 2 sts together & turn; (WS) purl to twin-wrapped sts, purl wrapped sts tog as one st, wrap 2 sts together & turn—2 sts decreased.

Rep this row until 1 st remains before each side marker.

Next short row *dec row:* (RS) Knit to twin-wrapped sts, knit wrapped sts tog as one st, wrap next *single* st, remove marker & turn; (WS) purl to twin-wrapped sts, purl wrapped sts tog as one st, wrap next *single* st, remove marker & turn—66 (72, 75, 81, 88, 93, 99, 106, 112, 116) sts.

Last row *dec row:* (RS) Knit to prev wrapped st, k2tog-tbl with next st, k2 (4, 4, 5, 6, 6, 7, 10, 11, 11)—65 (71, 74, 80, 87, 92, 98, 105, 111, 115) sts.

Work sleeve in the round

Rnd 1 *dec rnd:* K2 (4, 4, 5, 6, 6, 7, 10, 11, 11), k2tog with remaining wrapped st, knit to end of round—64 (70, 73, 79, 86, 91, 97, 104, 110, 114) sts.

Next 6 rnds: Knit.

Change to preferred needle style for small circumference knitting in the round when necessary.

Next rnd *dec rnd:* K1, ssk, knit to last 3 sts, k2tog, k1—2 sts decreased.

Work *dec rnd* every 7th (6th, 6th, 5th, 5th, 5th, 5th, 4th, 4th) rnd 4 (5, 5, 6, 17, 18, 7, 7, 24, 26) more times, then every 10th (8th, 8th, 6th, –, –, 4th, 4th, –, –) rnd 5 (7, 7, 9, –, –, 14, 16, –, –) more times—44 (44, 47, 47, 50, 53, 53, 56, 60, 60) sts.

Work even until sleeve measures approx 11¼ (11¾, 11¾, 12¼, 12¼, 12¾, 12¾, 13¼, 13¼, 13¾)" [28.5 (30, 30, 31, 31, 32.5, 32.5, 33.5, 33.5, 35) cm] from underarm, or desired length, less 5¼" [13 cm].

Right cuff

Set-up Rnd 1: Remove marker, k8 (8, 6, 6, 5, 3, 3, 2, 16, 16), **pm** for new beginning of round, k13 (13, 16, 16, 19, 22, 22, 25, 13, 13), **pm**, knit to end.

Set-up Rnd 2: Knit.

Left cuff

Set-up Rnd 1: Remove marker, k23 (23, 24, 24, 26, 27, 27, 29, 31, 31), **pm** for new beginning of round, k13 (13, 16, 16, 19, 22, 22, 25, 13, 13), **pm**, knit to end.

Both cuffs

Establish slip-stitch panel.

Rnd 1: Sl 1, [k2, sl 1] 4 (4, 5, 5, 6, 7, 7, 8, 4, 4) times, **sl m**, knit to end.

Rnd 2: K1-tbl, [k2, k1-tbl] 4 (4, 5, 5, 6, 7, 7, 8, 4, 4) times, **sl m**, knit to end.

Rep these two rnds four more times.

Continue working slip-stitch panel as established, and begin working cuff pattern over remaining 31 (31, 31, 31, 31, 31, 31, 31, 47, 47) sts between markers (see page 63 for written instructions and chart).

Next rnd: Work slip-stitch panel to marker, **sl m**, work Rnd 1 of cuff pattern.

Next 3 rnds: Work slip-stitch panel to marker, **sl m**, work next rnd of cuff pattern.

Rep these four rnds seven more times.

Twisted ribbing

Rnd 1: Purl.

Rnd 2: If stitch count is odd number, k2tog; knit to end.

Rnds 3–5: [K1-tbl, p1] to end.

Bind off all stitches in pattern.

FINISHING

Weave in all ends. Block sweater to measurements.

line-by-line instructions for stitch patterns

Front Panel, sizes 51, 53½ and 57"
[129.5, 136 and 145 cm]

Row 1: (RS) [K3, p1] twice, sl 1, * p1, k3, p1, k2, sl 1, k2, p1, k3, p1, sl 1; rep from *, end [p1, k3] twice.

Row 2: P2, k1, p3, k1, p1, * [p1-tbl, p1, k1, p3, k1, p1] twice; rep from *, end p1-tbl, p1, k1, p3, k1, p2.

Row 3: K1, p1, k3, p1, k2, sl 1, * k2, p1, k3, p1, sl 1, p1, k3, p1, k2, sl 1; rep from *, end k2, p1, k3, p1, k1.

Row 4: [K1, p3] twice, * [p1-tbl, p3, k1, p3] twice; rep from *, end p1-tbl, [p3, k1] twice.

Front Panel, sizes 45¼ and 48"
[115 and 122 cm]

Row 1: (RS) K2, p1, k3, p1, sl 1, * p1, k3, p1, k2, sl 1, k2, p1, k3, p1, sl 1; rep from *, end p1, k3, p1, k2.

Row 2: P1, k1, p3, k1, p1, * [p1-tbl, p1, k1, p3, k1, p1] twice; rep from *, end p1-tbl, p1, k1, p3, k1, p1.

Row 3: P1, k3, p1, k2, sl 1, * k2, p1, k3, p1, sl 1, p1, k3, p1, k2, sl 1; rep from *, end k2, p1, k3, p1.

Row 4: P3, k1, p3, * [p1-tbl, p3, k1, p3] twice; rep from *, end p1-tbl, p3, k1, p3.

Front Panel, sizes 36¼, 38½ and 42"
[92, 97.5 and 106.5 cm]

Row 1: (RS) K1, p1, k3, p1, sl 1, * p1, k3, p1, k2, sl 1, k2, p1, k3, p1, sl 1; rep from *, end p1, k3, p1, k1.

Row 2: K1, p3, k1, p1, * [p1-tbl, p1, k1, p3, k1, p1] twice; rep from *, end p1-tbl, p1, k1, p3, k1.

Row 3: K3, p1, k2, sl 1, * k2, p1, k3, p1, sl 1, p1, k3, p1, k2, sl 1; rep from *, end k2, p1, k3.

Row 4: P2, k1, p3, * [p1-tbl, p3, k1, p3] twice; rep from *, end p1-tbl, p3, k1, p2.

Front Panel, sizes 30¼ and 32½"
[76.5 and 82.5 cm]

Row 1: (RS) P1, k3, p1, sl 1, * p1, k3, p1, k2, sl 1, k2, p1, k3, p1, sl 1; rep from *, end p1, k3, p1.

Row 2: P3, k1, p1, * [p1-tbl, p1, k1, p3, k1, p1] twice; rep from *, end p1-tbl, p1, k1, p3.

Row 3: K2, p1, k2, sl 1, * k2, p1, k3, p1, sl 1, p1, k3, p1, k2, sl 1; rep from *, end k2, p1, k2.

Row 4: P1, k1, p3, * [p1-tbl, p3, k1, p3] twice; rep from *, end p1-tbl, p3, k1, p1.

Hem, size 38½ and 53½"
[97.5 136 cm]

Rnd 1: [K3, p1] twice, sl 1, * p1, k3, p1, k2, sl 1, k2, p1, k3, p1, sl 1; rep from *, end [p1, k3] twice.

Rnd 2: K2, p1, k3, p1, k1, k1-tbl, * [k1, p1, k3, p1, k1, k1-tbl] twice; rep from *, end k1, p1, k3, p1, k2.

Rnd 3: K1, p1, k3, p1, k2, sl 1, * k2, p1, k3, p1, sl 1, p1, k3, p1, k2, sl 1; rep from *, end k2, p1, k3, p1, k1.

Rnd 4: [P1, k3] twice, k1-tbl, * [k3, p1, k3, k1-tbl] twice; rep from *, end [k3, p1] twice.

Hem, sizes 32½, 45¼ and 51"
[82.5, 115 and 129.5 cm]

Rnd 1: K2, p1, k3, p1, sl 1, * p1, k3, p1, k2, sl 1, k2, p1, k3, p1, sl 1; rep from *, end p1, k3, p1, k2.

Rnd 2: K1, p1, k3, p1, k1, k1-tbl, * [k1, p1, k3, p1, k1, k1-tbl] twice; rep from *, end k1, p1, k3, p1, k1.

Rnd 3: P1, k3, p1, k2, sl 1, * k2, p1, k3, p1, sl 1, p1, k3, p1, k2, sl 1; rep from *, end k2, p1, k3, p1.

Rnd 4: K3, p1, k3, k1-tbl, * [k3, p1, k3, k1-tbl] twice; rep from *, end k3, p1, k3.

Hem, size 30¼"
[76.5 cm]

Rnd 1: K1, p1, k3, p1, sl 1, * p1, k3, p1, k2, sl 1, k2, p1, k3, p1, sl 1; rep from *, end p1, k3, p1, k1.

Rnd 2: P1, k3, p1, k1, k1-tbl, * [k1, p1, k3, p1, k1, k1-tbl] twice; rep from *, end k1, p1, k3, p1.

Rnd 3: K3, p1, k2, sl 1, * k2, p1, k3, p1, sl 1, p1, k3, p1, k2, sl 1; rep from *, end k2, p1, k3.

Rnd 4: K2, p1, k3, k1-tbl, * [k3, p1, k3, k1-tbl] twice; rep from *, end k3, p1, k2.

Hem, sizes 36¼, 42 and 57"
[92, 106.5 and 145 cm]

Rnd 1: P1, k3, p1, sl 1, * p1, k3, p1, k2, sl 1, k2, p1, k3, p1, sl 1; rep from *, end p1, k3, p1.

Rnd 2: K3, p1, k1, k1-tbl, * [k1, p1, k3, p1, k1, k1-tbl] twice; rep from *, end k1, p1, k3.

Rnd 3: K2, p1, k2, sl 1, * k2, p1, k3, p1, sl 1, p1, k3, p1, k2, sl 1; rep from *, end k2, p1, k2.

Rnd 4: K1, p1, k3, k1-tbl, * [k3, p1, k3, k1-tbl] twice; rep from *, end k3, p1, k1.

Hem, size 48"
[122 cm]

Rnd 1: K2, p1, sl 1, * p1, k3, p1, k2, sl 1, k2, p1, k3, p1, sl 1; rep from *, end p1, k2.

Rnd 2: K1, p1, k1, k1-tbl, * [k1, p1, k3, p1, k1, k1-tbl] twice; rep from *, end k1, p1, k1.

Rnd 3: P1, k2, sl 1, * k2, p1, k3, p1, sl 1, p1, k3, p1, k2, sl 1; rep from *, end k2, p1.

Rnd 4: K3, k1-tbl, * [k3, p1, k3, k1-tbl] twice; rep from *, end k3.

stitch patterns, continued

Cuff, all sizes

Rnd 1: * P1, k3, p1, k2, sl 1, k2, p1, k3, p1, sl 1; rep from *, end p1, k3, p1, k2, sl 1, k2, p1, k3, p1.

Rnd 2: * [K1, p1, k3, p1, k1, k1-tbl] twice; rep from *, end k1, p1, k3, p1, k1, k1-tbl, k1, p1, k3, p1, k1.

Rnd 3: * K2, p1, k3, p1, sl 1, p1, k3, p1, k2, sl 1; rep from *, end k2, p1, k3, p1, sl 1, p1, k3, p1, k2.

Rnd 4: * [K3, p1, k3, k1-tbl] twice; rep from *, end k3, p1, k3, k1-tbl, k3, p1, k3.

Chart key

☐ knit on RS, purl on WS

● purl on RS, knit on WS

Ω knit-tbl on RS, purl-tbl on WS

V slip purlwise wyib on RS, wyif on WS

▢ pattern repeat

Front panel (worked flat)

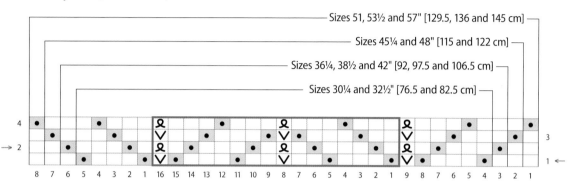

Hem (worked in the round)

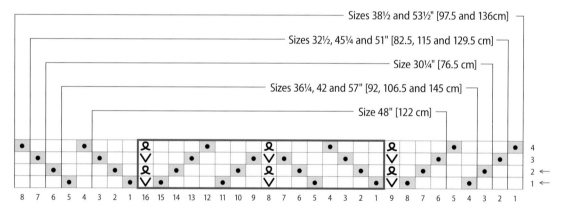

Cuff (worked in the round)

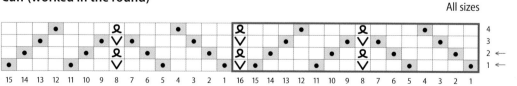

meris
Sock FW (handwritten)

Meris was my first published sweater pattern, and remains one of my favorite designs. It is being reprised here with updated sleeve cap and armhole shaping. Light and breezy, this cardigan is designed to fit with minimal ease at the bust, and bit of figure-skimming positive ease through the waist and hips. Geometric lace panels keep the knitting entertaining.

Finished measurements

Shoulder width: 12 (12¾, 13¼, 13¾, 14¼, 15¼, 16, 16¾, 17¼, 17¾)" [30.5 (32.5, 34, 34.5, 36, 38.5, 41, 42.5, 44, 45) cm]

Bust circumference: 29¾ (33, 36, 39, 41½, 44½, 47¾, 50¾, 53¼, 57)" [76.5 (84, 92, 100, 106, 114, 121.5, 129.5, 136, 145) cm]

Sample shown in 13¾" [34.5 cm] shoulder, 39" [100 cm] bust size.

Suggested ease at bust: -1 to +1" [-2.5 to +2.5 cm]

Materials
Fingering (handwritten)
Yarn

Finch by Quince & Co.
(100% American wool; 221 yd [202 m] / 50 g)

• 6 (6, 6, 7, 7, 7, 8, 8, 9, 9) skeins Aleutian (148)

Needles

Body
• US 3 [3.25 mm] circ, 32" [80 cm] long or longer

Bands
• US 1 [2.25 mm] circ, 24" [60 cm] long
• US 2 [2.75 mm] circ, 24" [60 cm] long

Sleeves
• US 3 [3.25 mm] circ, 16" [40 cm] long
• US 3 [3.25 mm] needles of preferred style for working small circumferences in the round

Or size to obtain gauge

Notions

• Waste yarn of similar gauge and contrasting color
• Stitch markers, both removable and fixed ring, including one unique
• Yarn needle
• Blocking wires and/or pins
• 5 or more ⁷⁄₁₆" [11 mm] buttons

Note: The buttonhole band has eyelet holes spaced approximately ³⁄₁₆" [5 mm] apart over its entire length. Buttons can be placed at whatever interval you desire. The sample has five buttons at the top, each spaced four eyelet holes apart.

Gauge

26 sts and 42 rows = 4" [10 cm] in stockinette stitch, worked flat on US 3 [3.25 mm] needles, after blocking.

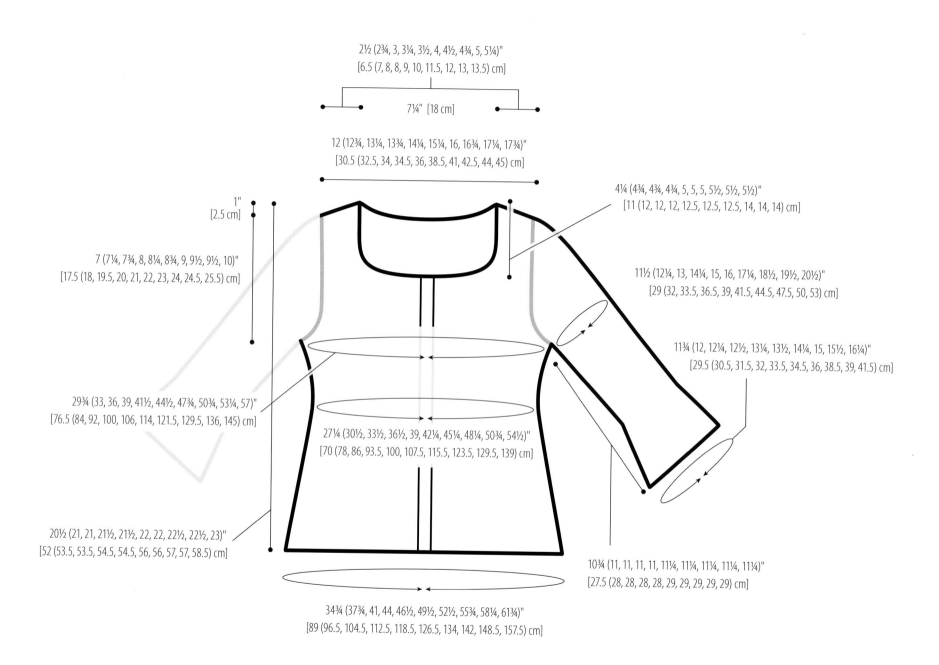

2½ (2¾, 3, 3¼, 3½, 4, 4½, 4¾, 5, 5¼)"
[6.5 (7, 8, 8, 9, 10, 11.5, 12, 13, 13.5) cm]

7¼" [18 cm]

12 (12¾, 13¼, 13¾, 14¼, 15¼, 16, 16¾, 17¼, 17¾)"
[30.5 (32.5, 34, 34.5, 36, 38.5, 41, 42.5, 44, 45) cm]

4¼ (4¾, 4¾, 4¾, 5, 5, 5, 5½, 5½, 5½)"
[11 (12, 12, 12, 12.5, 12.5, 12.5, 14, 14, 14) cm]

1"
[2.5 cm]

7 (7¼, 7¾, 8, 8¼, 8¾, 9, 9½, 9½, 10)"
[17.5 (18, 19.5, 20, 21, 22, 23, 24, 24.5, 25.5) cm]

11½ (12¼, 13, 14¼, 15, 16, 17¼, 18½, 19½, 20½)"
[29 (32, 33.5, 36.5, 39, 41.5, 44.5, 47.5, 50, 53) cm]

11¾ (12, 12¼, 12½, 13¼, 13½, 14¼, 15, 15½, 16¼)"
[29.5 (30.5, 31.5, 32, 33.5, 34.5, 36, 38.5, 39, 41.5) cm]

29¾ (33, 36, 39, 41½, 44½, 47¾, 50¾, 53¼, 57)"
[76.5 (84, 92, 100, 106, 114, 121.5, 129.5, 136, 145) cm]

27¼ (30½, 33½, 36½, 39, 42¼, 45¼, 48¼, 50¾, 54½)"
[70 (78, 86, 93.5, 100, 107.5, 115.5, 123.5, 129.5, 139) cm]

20½ (21, 21, 21½, 21½, 22, 22, 22½, 22½, 23)"
[52 (53.5, 53.5, 54.5, 54.5, 56, 56, 57, 57, 58.5) cm]

10¾ (11, 11, 11, 11, 11¼, 11¼, 11¼, 11¼, 11¼)"
[27.5 (28, 28, 28, 28, 29, 29, 29, 29, 29) cm]

34¾ (37¾, 41, 44, 46½, 49½, 52½, 55¾, 58¼, 61¾)"
[89 (96.5, 104.5, 112.5, 118.5, 126.5, 134, 142, 148.5, 157.5) cm]

BACK (begin at right shoulder)

With US 3 [3.25 mm] circ and the long-tail cast-on, loosely CO 18 (20, 22, 23, 25, 28, 31, 33, 35, 36) sts.

Set-up row: (WS) P1, k1, purl to end.

Shape right shoulder and back neck

Short Row 1: (RS) K4 (4, 4, 4, 5, 4, 4, 5, 6, 6), w&t; (WS) purl to end.

Short Row 2: (RS) K2, RLI, knit to wrapped st, pick up wrap, k2 (3, 3, 4, 4, 5, 6, 6, 6, 7), w&t; (WS) purl to end.

Short Row 3: Rep Short Row 2.

Short Row 4: (RS) Cable CO 2 sts, p2, knit to wrapped st, pick up wrap, k2 (3, 3, 4, 4, 5, 6, 6, 6, 7), w&t; (WS) purl to last 2 sts, k2.

Row 5: Cable CO 3 sts, k3, p2, knit to last 2 sts, picking up prev wrap, p1, k1.

Row 6: P1, k1, purl to last 5 sts, k2, p2, k1.

Row 7: Cable CO 2 sts, p2, k3, p2, knit to last 2 sts, p1, k1.

Row 8: P1, k1, purl to last 7 sts, k2, p3, k2—27 (29, 31, 32, 34, 37, 40, 42, 44, 45) sts.

Break yarn and slip stitches onto waste yarn.

Left shoulder

With US 3 [3.25 mm] circ and the long-tail cast-on, loosely CO 18 (20, 22, 23, 25, 28, 31, 33, 35, 36) sts.

Set-up Row 1: (WS) Purl to last 2 sts, k1, p1.

Set-up Row 2: K1, p1, knit to end.

Shape left shoulder and back neck

Short Row 1: (WS) P4 (4, 4, 4, 5, 4, 4, 5, 6, 6), w&t; (RS) knit to last 2 sts, LLI, k2.

Short Row 2: (WS) Purl to wrapped st, pick up wrap, p2 (3, 3, 4, 4, 5, 6, 6, 6, 7), w&t; (RS) knit to last 2 sts, LLI, k2.

Short Row 3: (WS) Purl to wrapped st, pick up wrap, p2 (3, 3, 4, 4, 5, 6, 6, 6, 7), w&t; (RS) knit to end, turn work and cable CO 2 sts.

Short Row 4: (WS) K2, purl to wrapped st, pick up wrap, p2 (3, 3, 4, 4, 5, 6, 6, 6, 7), w&t; (RS) knit to last 2 sts, p2, turn work and cable CO 3 sts.

Row 5: P3, k2, purl to last 2 sts, picking up prev wrap, k1, p1.

Row 6: K1, p1, knit to last 5 sts, p2, k3, turn work and cable CO 2 sts.

Row 7: K2, p3, k2, purl to last 2 sts, k1, p1—27 (29, 31, 32, 34, 37, 40, 42, 44, 45) sts.

Join shoulders

With RS facing, slip 27 (29, 31, 32, 34, 37, 40, 42, 44, 45) held right shoulder sts to left end of needle holding left shoulder sts.

Left shoulder: (RS) K1, p1, knit to last 7 sts, p2, k2tog, yo, k1, p2.

Back neck: Turn work to WS and cable CO 26 sts.

Right shoulder: Turn work to RS. Slip last st cast on back to LH needle, p2tog with first right shoulder st, p1, k2tog, yo, k1, p2, knit to last 2 sts, p1, k1—79 (83, 87, 89, 93, 99, 105, 109, 113, 115) sts.

Next row: (WS) P1, k1, p18 (20, 22, 23, 25, 28, 31, 33, 35, 36), pm, k2, p3, k2, p25, k2, p3, k2, pm, purl to last 2 sts, k1, p1.

Continue back and begin lace panel

Written instructions for lace patterns are found on page 74, charts on page 75.

Row 1: (RS) K1, p1, knit to marker, sl m, work Row 1 of back lace panel, sl m, knit to last 2 sts, p1, k1.

Row 2: P1, k1, purl to marker, sl m, work Row 2 of back lace panel, sl m, purl to last 2 sts, k1, p1.

Continue as established, working Rows 3–16 of back lace panel between markers, and maintaining purled 'gutter' at each end of piece.

Rep Rows 1–16 of back lace panel twice more, then work 8 (8, 8, 4, 6, 8, 10, 10, 8, 6) more rows of back lace panel. Piece should measure approx 6 (6, 6, 5½, 5¾, 6, 6¼, 6¼, 6, 5¾)" [15.5 (15.5, 15.5, 14.5, 15, 15.5, 16, 16, 15.5, 15) cm] from cast-on to bottom, measured at armhole edge.

Shape underarm

Next row inc row: (RS) K1, p1, k1, RLI, work in est patts to last 3 sts, LLI, k1, p1, k1—2 sts increased.

Next row: Work in est patts.

Rep these two rows 4 (4, 7, 10, 11, 11, 12, 14, 16, 19) more times—89 (93, 103, 111, 117, 123, 131, 139, 147, 155) sts.

Size 29¾" [76.5 cm]: skip to 'All sizes'
Sizes 33 to 57" [84 to 145 cm] only:

Next row: (RS) Cable CO – (2, 2, 2, 3, 2, 2, 2, 2, 3) sts, work in est patts to last 2 sts, p1, k1— – (95, 105, 113, 120, 125, 133, 141, 149, 158) sts.

Next row: Cable CO – (2, 2, 2, 3, 2, 2, 2, 2, 3) sts, work in est patts to second marker, purl to end— – (97, 107, 115, 123, 127, 135, 143, 151, 161) sts.

short row shaping

If you've never used them before, short rows may sound complicated, but really, they're not. Just as the name implies, a row is worked only part way across, then the piece is turned and worked back in the opposite direction. This adds fabric to the area where the extra rows are worked, allowing the garment to be shaped seamlessly.

To prevent a hole at the point of the turn, the working yarn must be anchored to the next stitch in the row before working back. There are numerous ways of anchoring the yarn, but the basic wrap and turn method is used here.

The wraps may later be hidden or not, depending on where in the garment they are used. For shoulder shaping in stockinette fabric, the wraps are 'picked up' by working them together with the stitch that they wrap. For the sleeve caps, the wraps are simply left in place and the wrapped stitch worked normally. The texture of the wraps blends into the sleeve seam.

wrap and turn method (w&t)

On the right side, bring the yarn to the front of work between the needles. Slip the next stitch to the right needle and take the yarn to the back of the work, wrapping the yarn in front of the stitch. Slip stitch back to the left needle. Turn, and work next row.

On the wrong side, take the yarn to the back of the work between the needles. Slip the next

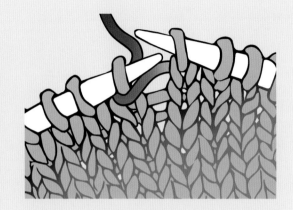

stitch to the right needle and bring the yarn to the front of the work, wrapping the yarn behind the stitch. Slip stitch back to left needle. Turn and work next row.

Make the wraps as tight as possible to keep the transition smooth. Depending on how you tension your yarn, you may find that slipping the stitch before shifting the position of the working yarn gives you a tighter wrap, or vice versa.

picking up wraps

(RS) Insert the right needle tip into the wrap from below, front to back, then into the stitch that it wraps, and knit the two together, making sure that the wrap falls to the wrong side of the work.

(WS) Insert the right needle tip into the wrap from below, back to front, lifting it over the stitch that it wraps, and purl the two together, making sure that the wrap falls to the wrong side of work.

For more information, watch this short row video tutorial: https://vimeo.com/128883334

Sizes 33 to 41½" [84 to 106 cm]: skip to 'All sizes'
Sizes 44½ to 57" [114 to 145 cm] only:

Next row: (RS) Cable CO – (–, –, –, –, 2, 2, 3, 3, 3) sts, work in est patts to end— – (–, –, –, –, 129, 137, 146, 154, 164) sts.

Next row: Cable CO – (–, –, –, –, 2, 2, 3, 3, 3) sts, work in est patts to end— – (–, –, –, –, 131, 139, 149, 157, 167) sts.

All sizes

Piece should measure approx 7 (7¼, 7¾, 8, 8¼, 8¾, 9, 9½, 9½, 10)" [18 (18.5, 20, 20.5, 21.5, 22.5, 23, 24, 24.5, 25.5) cm] from cast-on to bottom, measured at armhole edge.

Break yarn and slip stitches onto waste yarn.

FRONTS

Pick up for right front shoulder

With RS facing, attach yarn at armhole edge of right shoulder. With US 3 [3.25 mm] circ, pick up and knit 17 (19, 21, 22, 24, 27, 30, 32, 34, 35) stitches along cast-on edge.

Set-up Row 1: (WS) Purl to last 2 sts, k1, p1.

Set-up Row 2: K1, p1, knit to end.

Shape right front shoulder

Short Row 1: (WS) P3 (3, 3, 3, 4, 3, 3, 4, 5, 5), w&t; (RS) knit to end.

Short Row 2: (WS) Purl to wrapped st, pick up wrap, p2 (3, 3, 4, 4, 5, 6, 6, 6, 7), w&t; (RS) knit to end.

Short Rows 3 & 4: Rep Short Row 2.

Row 5: Purl to last 2 sts, picking up prev wrap, k1, p1.

Tie a yarn marker around the last stitch of the row just worked.

Work even, maintaining purled 'gutter' at armhole edge, until 26 (30, 30, 30, 34, 34, 34, 38, 38, 38) rows have been worked from yarn marker. Piece should measure approx 2¾ (3¼, 3¼, 3¼, 3½, 3½, 3½, 4, 4, 4)" [7 (8, 8, 8, 9, 9, 9, 10, 10, 10) cm] from cast-on to bottom, measured at armhole edge.

Shape right front neckline

Row 1: (RS) K1, p1, knit to last 2 sts, LLI, k2—18 (20, 22, 23, 25, 28, 31, 33, 35, 36) sts.

Row 2: Purl to last 2 sts, k1, p1.

Row 3: K1, p1, knit to end.

Row 4: Cable CO 2 sts, k2, purl to last 2 sts, k1, p1—20 (22, 24, 25, 27, 30, 33, 35, 37, 38) sts.

Row 5: K1, p1, knit to last 2 sts, p2.

Row 6: Cable CO 3 sts, p3, k2, purl to last 2 sts, k1, p1—23 (25, 27, 28, 30, 33, 36, 38, 40, 41) sts.

Row 7: K1, p1, knit to last 5 sts, p2, k3.

Row 8: Cable CO 2 sts, k2, p3, k2, purl to last 2 sts, k1, p1—25 (27, 29, 30, 32, 35, 38, 40, 42, 43) sts.

Row 9: K1, p1, knit to last 7 sts, p2, k2tog, yo, k1, p2.

Row 10: Cable CO 15 sts, p1, k1, p13, k2, p3, k2, **pm**, purl to last 2 sts, k1, p1—40 (42, 44, 45, 47, 50, 53, 55, 57, 58) sts.

Continue right front

Next row: (RS) K1, p1, knit to marker, **sl m**, work Row 1 (5, 5, 5, 9, 9, 9, 13, 13, 13) of right front lace panel.

Next row: Work next row of right front lace panel, **sl m**, purl to last 2 sts, k1, p1.

Continue as established, through Row 16 of right front lace panel, and maintaining purled 'gutter' at armhole edge, then work 8 (8, 8, 4, 6, 8, 10, 10, 8, 6) more rows of right front lace panel. End having worked a WS row.

Piece should measure approx 6 (6, 6, 5½, 5¾, 6, 6¼, 6¼, 6, 5¾)" [15.5 (15.5, 15.5, 14.5, 15, 15.5, 16, 16, 15.5, 15) cm] from shoulder seam to bottom, measured at armhole edge.

Shape underarm

Next row *inc row:* (RS) K1, p1, k1, RLI, work in est patts to end—1 st increased.

Next row: (WS) Work in est patts.

Rep these two rows 4 (4, 7, 10, 11, 11, 12, 14, 16, 19) more times—45 (47, 52, 56, 59, 62, 66, 70, 74, 78) sts.

Size 29¾" [76.5 cm]: skip to 'All sizes'
Sizes 33 to 57" [84 to 145 cm] only:

Next row: (RS) Cable CO – (2, 2, 2, 3, 2, 2, 2, 2, 3) sts, work in est patts to end— – (49, 54, 58, 62, 64, 68, 72, 76, 81) sts.

Next row: Work in est patts.

Sizes 33 to 41½" [84 to 106 cm]: skip to 'All sizes'
Sizes 44½ to 57" [114 to 145 cm] only:

Next row: (RS) Cable CO – (–, –, –, –, 2, 2, 3, 3, 3) sts, work in est patts to end— – (–, –, –, –, 66, 70, 75, 79, 84) sts.

Next row: Work in est patts.

All sizes

Piece should measure approx 7 (7¼, 7¾, 8, 8¼, 8¾, 9, 9½, 9½, 10)" [17.5 (18, 19.5, 20, 21, 22, 23, 24, 24.5, 25.5) cm] from shoulder seam to bottom, measured at armhole edge.

Break yarn and slip stitches onto waste yarn.

Pick up for left front shoulder

With RS facing, attach yarn at neck edge of left shoulder. With US 3 [3.25 mm] circ, pick up and knit 17 (19, 21, 22, 24, 27, 30, 32, 34, 35) stitches along cast-on edge.

Set-up row: (WS) P1, k1, purl to end.

Shape left front shoulder

Short Row 1: (RS) K3 (3, 3, 3, 4, 3, 3, 4, 5, 5), w&t; (WS) purl.

Short Row 2: (RS) Knit to wrapped st, pick up wrap, k2 (3, 3, 4, 4, 5, 6, 6, 6, 7), w&t; (WS) purl.

Short Rows 3 & 4: Rep Short Row 2.

Row 5: Knit to last 2 sts, picking up prev wrap, p1, k1.

Row 6: P1, k1, purl to end.

Tie a yarn marker around the last stitch of the row just worked.

Work even, maintaining purled 'gutter' at armhole edge, until 26 (30, 30, 30, 34, 34, 34, 38, 38, 38) rows have been worked from yarn marker. Piece should measure approx 2¾ (3¼, 3¼, 3¼, 3½, 3½, 3½, 4, 4, 4)" [7 (8, 8, 8, 9, 9, 9, 10, 10, 10) cm] from shoulder seam to bottom, measured at armhole edge.

Shape left front neckline

Row 1: (RS) K2, RLI, knit to last 2 sts, p1, k1—18 (20, 22, 23, 25, 28, 31, 33, 35, 36) sts.

Row 2: P1, k1, purl to end.

Row 3: Cable CO 2 sts, p2, knit to last 2 sts, p1, k1—20 (22, 24, 25, 27, 30, 33, 35, 37, 38) sts.

Row 4: P1, k1, purl to last 2 sts, k2.

Row 5: Cable CO 3 sts, k3, p2, knit to last 2 sts, p1, k1—23 (25, 27, 28, 30, 33, 36, 38, 40, 41) sts.

Row 6: P1, k1, purl to last 5 sts, k2, p2, k1.

Row 7: Cable CO 2 sts, p2, k3, p2, knit to last 2 sts, p1, k1—25 (27, 29, 30, 32, 35, 38, 40, 42, 43) sts.

Row 8: P1, k1, purl to last 7 sts, k2, p3, k2.

Break yarn, leaving an 8" [20 cm] tail.

Using the long-tail cast-on, CO 16 sts to empty end of needle. With RS facing, sl last CO st to LH needle, and purl it together with the first left front st. Work across remaining sts as follows:

Row 9: (RS) P1, k2tog, yo, k1, p2, knit to last 2 sts, p1, k1—40 (42, 44, 45, 47, 50, 53, 55, 57, 58) sts.

Row 10: P1, k1, p16 (18, 20, 21, 23, 26, 29, 31, 33, 34), **pm**, k2, p3, k2, p13, k1, p1.

Continue left front

Next row: (RS) Work Row 1 (5, 5, 5, 9, 9, 13, 13, 13) of left front lace panel, **sl m**, knit to last 2 sts, p1, k1.

Next row: (WS) P1, k1, purl to marker, **sl m**, work next row of left front lace panel.

Continue as established, through Row 16 of left front lace panel, and maintaining purled 'gutter' at armhole edge, then work 8 (8, 8, 4, 6, 8, 10, 10, 8, 6) more rows of left front lace panel. End having worked a WS row.

Piece should measure approx 6 (6, 6, 5½, 5¾, 6, 6¼, 6¼, 6, 5¾)" [15.5 (15.5, 15.5, 14.5, 15, 15.5, 16, 16, 15.5, 15) cm] from shoulder seam to bottom, measured at armhole edge.

Shape underarm

Next row *inc row:* (RS) Work in est patts to last 3 sts, LLI, k1, p1, k1.

Next row: Work in est patts.

Rep these two rows 4 (4, 7, 10, 11, 11, 12, 14, 16, 19) more times—45 (47, 52, 56, 59, 62, 66, 70, 74, 78) sts.

Size 29¾" [76.5 cm]: skip to 'All sizes'
Sizes 33 to 57" [84 to 145 cm] only:

Next row: (RS) Work in est patts.

Next row: Cable CO – (2, 2, 2, 3, 2, 2, 2, 2, 3) sts, work in est patts to end— – (49, 54, 58, 62, 64, 68, 72, 76, 81) sts.

Sizes 33 to 41½" [84 to 106 cm]: skip to 'All sizes'
Sizes 44½ to 57" [114 to 145 cm] only:

Next row: (RS) Work in est patts.

Next row: Cable CO – (–, –, –, –, 2, 2, 3, 3, 3) sts, work in est patts to end— – (–, –, –, –, 66, 70, 75, 79, 84) sts.

All sizes

Piece should measure approx 7 (7¼, 7¾, 8, 8¼, 8¾, 9, 9½, 9½, 10)" [17.5 (18, 19.5, 20, 21, 22, 23, 24, 24.5, 25.5) cm] from shoulder seam to bottom, measured at armhole edge.

Join fronts to back

With RS facing, slip 89 (97, 107, 115, 123, 131, 139, 149, 157, 167) held back stitches to left end of needle holding left front sts, then slip 45 (49, 54, 58, 62, 66, 70, 75, 79, 84) held right front sts to needle.

Left Front: (RS) Work Row 3 (5, 11, 13, 1, 5, 9, 13, 15, 3) of left front lace panel, **sl m**, knit to end. Turn work to WS and cable CO 7 (9, 9, 11, 11, 13, 15, 15, 15, 17) sts.

Back: Turn work to RS. Slip last st cast on back to LH needle, k2tog with first back st. Knit across back sts to marker, **sl m**, work Row 3 (5, 11, 13, 1, 5, 9, 13, 15, 3) of back lace panel, **sl m**, knit to end. Turn work to WS and cable CO 7 (9, 9, 11, 11, 13, 15, 15, 15, 17) sts.

Right front: Turn work to RS. Slip last st cast on back to LH needle, k2tog with first right front st. Knit across right front sts to marker, **sl m**, work Row 3 (5, 11, 13, 1, 5, 9, 13, 15, 3) of right front lace panel—191 (211, 231, 251, 267, 287, 307, 327, 343, 367) sts.

Next row: (WS) Work next row of right front lace panel, **sl m**, purl to marker, **sl m**, work next row of back lace panel, **sl m**, purl to marker, **sl m**, work next row of left front lace panel.

BODICE

Continue working in est patts, until sweater reaches apex of bust. End having worked a WS row.

Underbust decrease set-up

Four additional markers are placed to indicate position of waist shaping darts. Front markers should be in line with, or just slightly to the outside of bust points.

Next row *place markers:* (RS) * Work in patt to marker, **sl m**, k4 (4, 4, 6, 6, 8, 8, 10, 10, 12), **pm**, knit to 4 (4, 4, 6, 6, 8, 8, 10, 10, 12) sts before next marker, **pm**, k4 (4, 4, 6, 6, 8, 8, 10, 10, 12), **sl m**; rep from * once more, then work in patt to end—4 dart markers added.

Continue working in est patts until bodice is approx ½ to 1" [1.5 to 2.5 cm] below apex of bust. End having worked a WS row.

Begin underbust decreases

Next row *dec row:* (RS) Work in est patts to first dart marker, **sl m**, k2tog, knit to 2 sts before second dart marker, ssk, **sl m**, work in est patts to third dart marker, **sl m**, k2tog, knit to 2 sts before fourth dart marker, ssk, **sl m**, work in est patts to end—4 sts decreased.

Next 3 rows: Work even as est.

Rep these four rows three more times—175 (195, 215, 235, 251, 271, 291, 311, 327, 351) sts.

Continue working in est patts until sweater is approx ¾ to 1" [2 to 2.5 cm] above waistline or narrowest part of torso. End having worked a WS row, then place four secondary dart markers as follows:

Next row *place markers:* (RS) Work in est patts to first dart marker, **sl m**, k4, **pm**, knit to 4 sts before next dart marker, **pm**, work in est patts to third dart marker, **sl m**, k4, **pm**, knit to 4 sts before fourth dart marker, **pm**, work in est patts to end—4 markers added, 8 dart markers total.

Next row: Work in est patts.

SKIRT
Begin hip increases

Next row *inc row:* (RS) * Work in est patts to first dart marker, LLI, **sl m**, knit to second dart marker, LLI, **sl m**, knit to third dart marker, **sl m**, RLI, knit to fourth dart marker, **sl m**, RLI; rep from * through next four dart markers, work in est patts to end—8 sts increased.

skirt shaping

As written, the pattern's waist shaping instructions give a slight peplum flare to the skirt. If you prefer, this flare can be reduced by omitting the placement of the second set of markers for the hip increases and working only those increases that are in line with the underbust decreases.

For a straighter shape still, work one pair of increases on the back of the garment and no increases on the front.

Next 3 rows: Work even in est patts.

Rep these four rows three more times. When final *inc row* is complete, remove the four secondary dart markers—207 (227, 247, 267, 283, 303, 323, 343, 359, 383) sts.

Next row *inc row:* * Work in est patts to first dart marker, LLI, **sl m**, knit to second dart marker, **sl m**, RLI; rep from * through next two dart markers, work in est patts to end—4 sts increased.

Next 3 rows: Work even in est patts.

Work these four rows three more times—223 (243, 263, 283, 299, 319, 339, 359, 375, 399) sts.

Work even in est patts until sweater measures 20⅛ (20⅝, 20⅝, 21⅛, 21⅛, 21⅝, 21⅝, 22⅛, 22⅛, 22⅝)" [51 (52.5, 52.5, 53.5, 53.5, 55, 55, 56, 56, 57.5) cm] from neck edge to bottom, or desired length, less ⅜" [1 cm]. End having worked a WS row. Do not break yarn.

I-cord bind-off

Bind-off row: (RS) CO 4 sts to LH needle using the knitted cast-on method. K3, k2tog-tbl with st from body, * sl 4 sts back to LH needle, pull yarn firmly across back of work, k3, k2tog-tbl; rep from * until 1 body st remains.

Last row: K2tog, k1, k2tog-tbl with last st from body of sweater—3 sts remain.

Slip remaining stitches to holder. Leave working yarn attached.

BANDS

Button band

Using a separate ball of yarn, attach yarn at neck edge of left front. With US 1 [2.25 mm] circ, pick up and knit approx 3 stitches for every 4 rows along left front edge. Make a note of the number of stitches picked up.

Row 1: (WS) Purl.

Row 2: * Yo, k2tog-tbl, sl st just worked back to LH needle; rep from *, ending k2tog-tbl.

Row 3: Knit-tbl.

Rows 4–10: Knit.

Bind off all stitches purlwise.

Buttonhole band

Return 3 held stitches to US 1 [2.25 mm] circ. With attached yarn, pick up and knit stitches as for button band, making sure to pick up the same number of stitches.

Row 1: (WS) Purl.

Row 2: * Yo, k2tog-tbl, sl st just worked back to LH needle; rep from *, ending k2tog-tbl.

Row 3: Knit-tbl.

Change to US 2 [2.75 mm] circ.

Row 4: Knit.

Row 5: P1, * p1, yo, p2tog; rep from * to ⅜" [1 cm] from end of band, purl to end.

Row 6: Knit.

Change to US 1 [2.25 mm] circ.

Rows 7–9: Knit.

Bind off all stitches. Do not break yarn—1 st remains.

I-cord neckband

Counting remaining st as first st, pick up and knit 5 more sts across top of buttonhole band, 21 sts across right front neck, 36 (39, 39, 39, 42, 42, 42, 45, 45, 45) sts along right vertical edge of neck, 39 sts along back neck, 36 (39, 39, 39, 42, 42, 42, 45, 45, 45) sts along left vertical edge of neck, 21 sts across left front neck, and 6 more sts across top of button band—165 (171, 171, 171, 177, 177, 177, 183, 183, 183) sts.

Change to US 3 [3.25 mm] circ.

Row 1: (WS) Knit.

Bind-off row: (RS) CO 3 sts to LH needle using the knitted cast-on method. K2, k2tog-tbl with st from body, * sl 3 sts back to LH needle, pull yarn firmly across back of work, k2, k2tog-tbl; rep from * until all neckband sts have been worked. Sl 3 sts back to LH needle, k2tog, then bind off remaining sts.

Break yarn, leaving a 6" [15 cm] tail. Thread tail onto yarn needle and pass needle into I-cord tube. Snake needle through for 2" [5 cm], then bring yarn needle out back side of work, pulling yarn tight to square up end of neckband. Repeat for other end of neckband.

SLEEVES

Note: Pick up stitches using US 1 [2.25 mm] needle, then transfer them to 16" [40 cm] long US 3 [3.25 mm] circ before beginning to work sleeve cap.

Place a removable stitch marker on front and back 1⅛ (1¼, 1¼, 1⅜, 1½, 1⅝, 1¾, 1⅞, 2, 2⅛)" [2.75 (3, 3.25, 3.5, 3.75, 4, 4.5, 4.75, 5, 5.5) cm] away from the shoulder seam. Place a third marker at the center of the underarm. The marker to right of shoulder seam is **M-one**, to left of shoulder is **M-two**, at underarm is **M-three**.

Begin at **M-one**. Working just inside the column of knit sts on the edge of armhole, pick up and knit 20 (20, 22, 24, 26, 26, 30, 32, 36, 38) sts between **M-one** and **M-two**, pick up and knit 31 (31, 32, 34, 35, 36, 37, 39, 40, 41) sts between **M-two** and the cast-on sts at underarm, **pm**, pick up and knit 1 st in each of the 3 (6, 6, 7, 8, 10, 11, 12, 12, 14) cast-on sts before **M-three**, place unique marker for beginning of round, pick up and knit 1 st in each of the remaining 3 (6, 6, 7, 8, 10, 11, 12, 12, 14) cast-on sts at underarm, **pm**, pick up and knit 31 (31, 32, 34, 35, 36, 37, 39, 40, 41) more sts, ending at **M-one**—88 (94, 98, 106, 112, 118, 126, 134, 140, 148) sts.

Remove **M-one**, **M-two** and **M-three**.

Shape upper cap

When working the short rows that shape the sleeve caps, the wraps are not picked up; they are left in place and the wrapped stitch is worked in the normal fashion.

Short Row 1: (RS) K20 (20, 22, 24, 26, 26, 30, 32, 36, 38), w&t; (WS) p20 (20, 22, 24, 26, 26, 30, 32, 36, 38), w&t.

Short Row 2: (RS) Knit to prev wrapped st, knit wrapped st, sl 1 wyif, shift yarn to back, w&t; (WS) purl to prev wrapped st, purl wrapped st, sl 1 wyib, bring yarn to front, w&t.

Rep Short Row 2 twice more.

Shape mid cap

Next short row: (RS) Knit to prev wrapped st, knit wrapped st, w&t; (WS) purl to prev wrapped st, purl wrapped st, w&t.

Rep this row, working back and forth to build the sleeve cap, until 11 sts remain before each of the side markers that separate the underarm sts from the sleeve cap.

Shape lower cap

Next short row: (RS) Knit to prev wrapped st, knit wrapped st, then wrap the next 2 sts together & turn; (WS) purl to prev wrapped st, purl wrapped st, then wrap the next 2 sts together & turn.

Next short row *dec row:* (RS) Knit to twin-wrapped sts, knit wrapped sts tog as one st, wrap 2 sts together & turn; (WS) purl to twin-wrapped sts, purl wrapped sts tog as one st, wrap 2 sts together & turn—2 sts decreased.

Rep this row until 1 st remains before each side marker.

Next short row *dec row:* (RS) Knit to twin-wrapped sts, knit wrapped sts tog as one st, wrap next *single* st, remove marker & turn; (WS) purl to twin-wrapped sts, purl wrapped sts tog as one st, wrap next *single* st, remove marker & turn—78 (84, 88, 96, 102, 108, 116, 124, 130, 138) sts.

Last row *dec row:* (RS) Knit to prev wrapped st, k2tog-tbl with next st, k2 (5, 5, 6, 7, 9, 10, 11, 11, 13)—77 (83, 87, 95, 101, 107, 115, 123, 129, 137) sts.

Work sleeve in the round

Rnd 1 *dec rnd:* K2 (5, 5, 6, 7, 9, 10, 11, 11, 13), k2tog with remaining wrapped st, knit to end of round—76 (82, 86, 94, 100, 106, 114, 122, 128, 136) sts.

Next 5 rnds: Knit.

Change to preferred needle style for small circumference knitting in the round when necessary.

Next rnd *dec rnd:* K1, ssk, knit to last 3 sts, k2tog, k1—2 sts decreased.

Work *dec rnd* every 11th (8th, 7th, 5th, 5th, 4th, 4th, 4th, 3rd, 3rd) rnd 5 (7, 8, 11, 12, 14, 16, 17, 19, 20) more times, then work even until sleeve reaches crease of elbow—64 (66, 68, 70, 74, 76, 80, 86, 88, 94) sts.

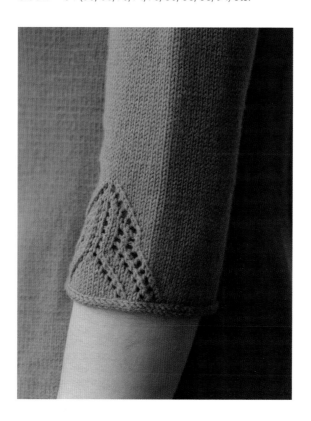

Lace cuff

Left sleeve set-up: K9 (9, 10, 11, 12, 13, 14, 16, 17, 19), **pm**, k27, **pm**, knit to end.

Right sleeve set-up: K28 (30, 31, 32, 35, 36, 39, 43, 44, 48), **pm**, k27, **pm**, knit to end.

Next rnd *inc rnd:* K1, RLI, knit to last st, LLI, k1—2 sts increased.

Next 5 rnds: Knit.

Rep these six rnds five more times.

At the same time, starting with the second *inc rnd*, begin working the sleeve insert pattern between markers. Work Rnds 1–28 of sleeve insert. See page 74 for written instructions, page 75 for chart—76 (78, 80, 82, 86, 88, 92, 98, 100, 106) sts.

Sleeve I-cord bind-off

Bind-off row: (RS) CO 3 sts to LH needle using the knitted cast-on method. K2, k2tog-tbl with st from body, * sl 3 sts back to LH needle, pull yarn firmly across back of work, k2, k2tog-tbl; rep from * until all sleeve sts have been worked. Sl 3 sts back to LH needle, k2tog, then bind off remaining sts.

Break yarn and pull through last st. Thread tail onto yarn needle, and sew ends of I-cord edging together.

FINISHING

Weave in all ends. Block sweater to measurements using pins and/or blocking wires to open up the lace pattern. Sew on buttons.

line-by-line instructions for lace patterns

Back panel *(39 sts and 16 rows)*

Row 1: (RS) P2, k3, p2, k1, yo, k2tog, k2, [k2tog, yo] twice, k1, k2tog, yo, k1, yo, ssk, k1, [yo, ssk] twice, k2, ssk, yo, k1, p2, k3, p2.

Row 2 and all other WS rows: K2, p3, k2, p25, k2, p3, k2.

Row 3: P2, k2tog, yo, k1, p2, k1, yo, k2tog, k1, [k2tog, yo] twice, k2, k2tog, yo, k1, yo, ssk, k2, [yo, ssk] twice, k1, ssk, yo, k1, p2, k2tog, yo, k1, p2.

Row 5: P2, k3, p2, k1, yo, k2tog, [k2tog, yo] twice, k2, k2tog, yo, k3, yo, ssk, k2, [yo, ssk] twice, ssk, yo, k1, p2, k3, p2.

Row 7: P2, k2tog, yo, k1, p2, k1, yo, k3tog, yo, k2tog, yo, k2, [k2tog, yo] twice, k1, [yo, ssk] twice, k2, yo, ssk, yo, sssk, yo, k1, p2, k2tog, yo, k1, p2.

Row 9: P2, k3, p2, k1, yo, k2tog twice, yo, k2, [k2tog, yo, k1] twice, yo, ssk, k1, yo, ssk, k2, yo, ssk twice, yo, k1, p2, k3, p2.

Row 11: P2, k2tog, yo, k1, p2, k1, [yo, k2tog] twice, k1, k2tog, yo, k2, k2tog, yo, k1, yo, ssk, k2, yo, ssk, k1, [ssk, yo] twice, k1, p2, k2tog, yo, k1, p2.

Row 13: P2, k3, p2, k1, yo, k2tog, k2, [k2tog, yo] twice, k1, k2tog, yo, k1, yo, ssk, k1, [yo, ssk] twice, k2, ssk, yo, k1, p2, k3, p2.

Row 15: P2, k2tog, yo, k1, p2, k1, yo, k2tog, k2, [k2tog, yo] twice, k1, k2tog, yo, k1, yo, ssk, k1, [yo, ssk] twice, k2, ssk, yo, k1, p2, k2tog, yo, k1, p2.

Row 16: (WS) K2, p3, k2, p25, k2, p3, k2.

Right front panel *(22 sts and 16 rows)*

Row 1: (RS) P2, k3, p2, k1, yo, ssk, k1, [yo, ssk] twice, k2, ssk, yo, k1, p1, k1.

Row 2 and all other WS rows: P1, k1, p13, k2, p3, k2.

Row 3: P2, k2tog, yo, k1, p2, k1, yo, ssk, k2, [yo, ssk] twice, k1, ssk, yo, k1, p1, k1.

Row 5: P2, k3, p2, [k2, yo, ssk] twice, yo, ssk twice, yo, k1, p1, k1.

Row 7: P2, k2tog, yo, k1, p2, k1, [yo, ssk] twice, k2, yo, ssk, yo, sssk, yo, k1, p1, k1.

Row 9: P2, k3, p2, [k1, yo, ssk] twice, k2, yo, ssk twice, yo, k1, p1, k1.

Row 11: P2, k2tog, yo, k1, p2, k1, yo, ssk, k2, yo, ssk, k1, [ssk, yo] twice, k1, p1, k1.

Row 13: P2, k3, p2, k1, yo, ssk, k1, [yo, ssk] twice, k2, ssk, yo, k1, p1, k1.

Row 15: P2, k2tog, yo, k1, p2, k1, yo, ssk, k1, [yo, ssk] twice, k2, ssk, yo, k1, p1, k1.

Row 16: (WS) P1, k1, p13, k2, p3, k2.

Left front panel *(22 sts and 16 rows)*

Row 1: (RS) K1, p1, k1, yo, k2tog, k2, [k2tog, yo] twice, k1, k2tog, yo, k1, p2, k3, p2.

Row 2 and all other WS rows: K2, p3, k2, p13, k1, p1.

Row 3: K1, p1, k1, yo, k2tog, k1, [k2tog, yo] twice, k2, k2tog, yo, k1, p2, k2tog, yo, k1, p2.

Row 5: K1, p1, k1, yo, k2tog twice, yo, [k2tog, yo, k2] twice, p2, k3, p2.

Row 7: K1, p1, k1, yo, k3tog, yo, k2tog, yo, k2, [k2tog, yo] twice, k1, p2, k2tog, yo, k1, p2.

Row 9: K1, p1, k1, yo, k2tog twice, yo, k2, [k2tog, yo, k1] twice, p2, k3, p2.

Row 11: K1, p1, k1, [yo, k2tog] twice, k1, k2tog, yo, k2, k2tog, yo, k1, p2, k2tog, yo, k1, p2.

Sleeve insert *(27 sts and 28 rnds)*

Rnd 1: K11, k2tog, yo, k1, yo, ssk, k11.

Rnd 2 and all other even-numbered rnds: Knit.

Rnd 3: K10, k2tog, yo, k3, yo, ssk, k10.

Rnd 5: K9, [k2tog, yo] twice, k1, [yo, ssk] twice, k9.

Rnd 7: K8, [k2tog, yo, k1] twice, yo, ssk, k1, yo, ssk, k8.

Rnd 9: K7, k2tog, yo, k2, k2tog, yo, k1, yo, ssk, k2, yo, ssk, k7.

Rnd 11: K6, [k2tog, yo] twice, k1, k2tog, yo, k1, yo, ssk, k1, [yo, ssk] twice, k6.

Rnds 13 & 15: Rep Rnd 11.

Rnd 17: K5, [k2tog, yo] twice, k2, k2tog, yo, k1, yo, ssk, k2, [yo, ssk] twice, k5.

Rnd 19: K4, [k2tog, yo] twice, k2, k2tog, yo, k3, yo, ssk, k2, [yo, ssk] twice, k4.

Rnd 21: K3, [k2tog, yo] twice, k2, k2tog, yo, k5, yo, ssk, k2, [yo, ssk] twice, k3.

Rnd 23: K2, [k2tog, yo] twice, k2, k2tog, yo, k7, yo, ssk, k2, [yo, ssk] twice, k2.

Rnd 25: K1, [k2tog, yo] twice, k2, k2tog, yo, k9, yo, ssk, k2, [yo, ssk] twice, k1.

Rnd 27: [K2tog, yo] twice, k2, k2tog, yo, k11, yo, ssk, k2, [yo, ssk] twice.

Rnd 28: Knit.

Back (worked flat)

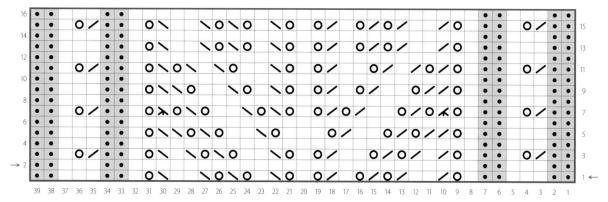

Right front (worked flat)

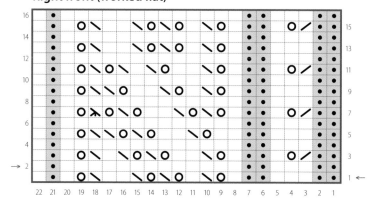

Left front (worked flat)

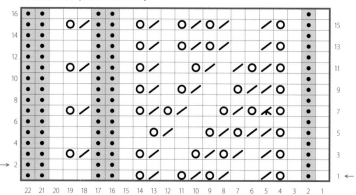

Sleeve insert (worked in the round)

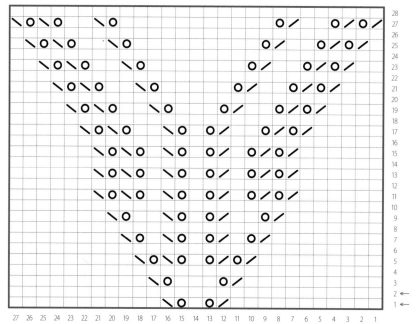

Chart key

	knit on RS, purl on WS
•	purl on RS, knit on WS
O	yarn over
/	k2tog
\	ssk
⋏	k3tog
⋌	sssk
▭	pattern repeat

copperplate

[handwritten: Between FW & sport]

An easy traveling rib stitch makes up the swirling motif that graces the fronts of this cozy cardi. The front bands are cast on separately then joined in and worked at the same time as the body. The fronts widen slightly toward the bottom for some gentle draping, and waist shaping within the side panels creates a flattering line. I-cord trim at cuffs and hem complement the edging pattern.

Finished measurements

Shoulder width: 12 (12¾, 13¼, 13¾, 14¼, 15¼, 16, 16¾, 17¼, 18)" [30.5 (32.5, 33.5, 35, 36.5, 38.5, 40.5, 42.5, 43.5, 45.5) cm]

Bust circumference: 30¾ (32½, 35¾, 38¼, 41¼, 43¾, 45¾, 48¾, 51¾, 55)" [78 (83, 90.5, 97, 105, 111.5, 116, 124, 131.5, 139.5) cm]

Note: Fronts do not meet at bustline. Measurements for bust circumference include the gap. For actual finished dimensions, see schematic, page 78.

Sample shown in 13¾" [35 cm] shoulder, 38¼" [97 cm] bust size.

Suggested ease at bust: Zero to +2" [0 to +5 cm]

Materials

[handwritten: Sport]

Yarn

Chickadee by Quince & Co.
(100% American wool; 181 yd [166 m] / 50 g)

• 8 (8, 8, 9, 9, 9, 10, 10, 11, 11) skeins Gingerbread (120)

Needles

Body
• US 7 [4.5 mm] circ, 32" [80 cm] long or longer
• US 7 [4.5 mm] set of dpns

Sleeves
• US 7 [4.5 mm] circ, 16" [40 cm] long
• US 7 [4.5 mm] needles of preferred style for working small circumferences in the round
• US 4 [3.5 mm] dpns or circ of any length, for I-cord bind off

Or size to obtain gauge

Optional
• US 2 [2.75 mm] circ, 32" [80 cm] long, for picking up stitches

Notions

• Waste yarn of a similar weight and contrasting color
• Crochet hook
• Stitch markers, both removable and fixed ring, including one unique
• Yarn needle

Gauge

21 sts and 32 rows = 4" [10 cm] in stockinette stitch, worked flat, on US 7 [4.5 mm] needles, after blocking.

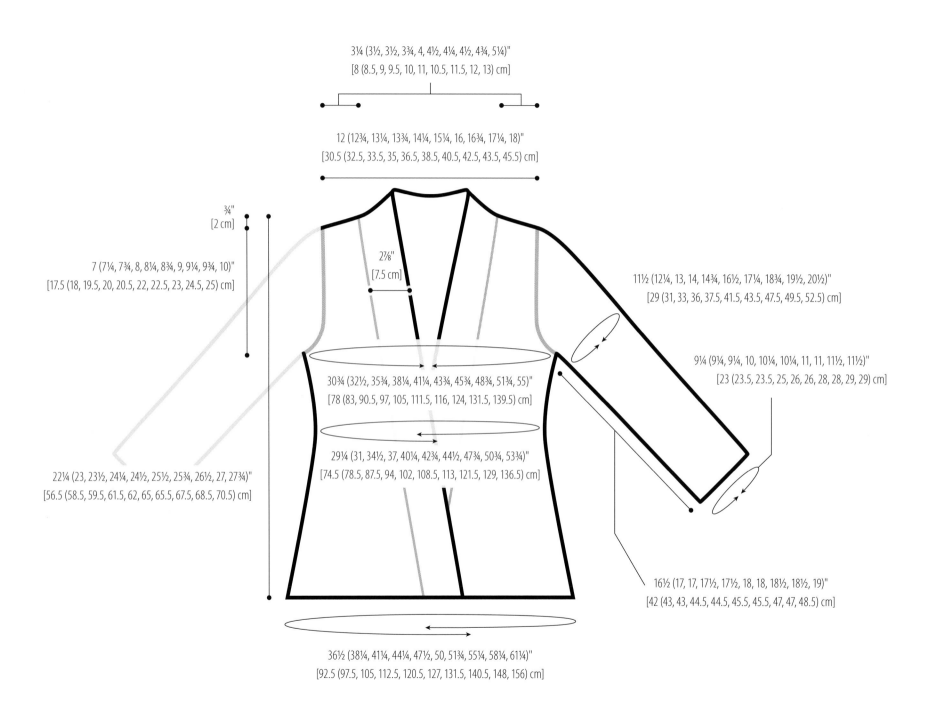

3¼ (3½, 3½, 3¾, 4, 4½, 4¼, 4½, 4¾, 5¼)"
[8 (8.5, 9, 9.5, 10, 11, 10.5, 11.5, 12, 13) cm]

12 (12¾, 13¼, 13¾, 14¼, 15¼, 16, 16¾, 17¼, 18)"
[30.5 (32.5, 33.5, 35, 36.5, 38.5, 40.5, 42.5, 43.5, 45.5) cm]

¾"
[2 cm]

7 (7¼, 7¾, 8, 8¼, 8¾, 9, 9¼, 9¾, 10)"
[17.5 (18, 19.5, 20, 20.5, 22, 22.5, 23, 24.5, 25) cm]

2⅞"
[7.5 cm]

11½ (12¼, 13, 14, 14¾, 16½, 17¼, 18¾, 19½, 20½)"
[29 (31, 33, 36, 37.5, 41.5, 43.5, 47.5, 49.5, 52.5) cm]

30¾ (32½, 35¾, 38¼, 41¼, 43¾, 45¾, 48¾, 51¾, 55)"
[78 (83, 90.5, 97, 105, 111.5, 116, 124, 131.5, 139.5) cm]

9¼ (9¼, 9¼, 10, 10¼, 10¼, 11, 11, 11½, 11½)"
[23 (23.5, 23.5, 25, 26, 26, 28, 28, 29, 29) cm]

29¼ (31, 34½, 37, 40¼, 42¾, 44½, 47¾, 50¾, 53¾)"
[74.5 (78.5, 87.5, 94, 102, 108.5, 113, 121.5, 129, 136.5) cm]

22¼ (23, 23½, 24¼, 24½, 25½, 25¾, 26½, 27, 27¾)"
[56.5 (58.5, 59.5, 61.5, 62, 65, 65.5, 67.5, 68.5, 70.5) cm]

16½ (17, 17, 17½, 17½, 18, 18, 18½, 18½, 19)"
[42 (43, 43, 44.5, 44.5, 45.5, 45.5, 47, 47, 48.5) cm]

36½ (38¼, 41¼, 44¼, 47½, 50, 51¾, 55¼, 58¼, 61¼)"
[92.5 (97.5, 105, 112.5, 120.5, 127, 131.5, 140.5, 148, 156) cm]

BACK (begin at right shoulder)

With US 7 [4.5 mm] dpns and the long-tail cast-on, loosely CO 19 (20, 21, 22, 23, 25, 24, 26, 27, 29) sts.

Set-up row: (WS) P1, k1, purl to end.

Shape right shoulder and back neck

Short Row 1: (RS) K4 (5, 4, 5, 5, 6, 6, 6, 6, 6), w&t; (WS) purl.

Short Row 2: (RS) K1, RLI, knit to wrapped st, pick up wrap, k4 (4, 5, 5, 5, 6, 5, 6, 6, 7), w&t; (WS) purl.

Short Row 3: Rep Short Row 2.

Row 4: Cable CO 3 sts, knit to last 2 sts, picking up wrap, p1, k1—24 (25, 26, 27, 28, 30, 29, 31, 32, 34) sts.

Row 5: (WS) P1, k1, purl to end.

Break yarn and set aside.

Left shoulder

Using US 7 [4.5 mm] circ and the long-tail cast-on, loosely CO 19 (20, 21, 22, 23, 25, 24, 26, 27, 29) sts.

Set-up Row 1: (WS) Purl to last 2 sts, k1, p1.

Set-up Row 2: K1, p1, knit to end.

Shape left shoulder and back neck

Short Row 1: (WS) P4 (5, 4, 5, 5, 6, 6, 6, 6, 6), w&t; (RS) knit to 1 st before end, LLI, k1.

Short Row 2: (WS) Purl to wrapped st, pick up wrap, p4 (4, 5, 5, 5, 6, 5, 6, 6, 7), w&t; (RS) knit to 1 st before end, LLI, k1.

Short Row 3: (WS) Purl to wrapped st, pick up wrap, p4 (4, 5, 5, 5, 6, 5, 6, 6, 7), w&t; (RS) knit to end.

Row 4: Cable CO 3 sts, purl to last 2 sts, picking up wrap, k1, p1—24 (25, 26, 27, 28, 30, 29, 31, 32, 34) sts.

Tie a yarn marker around the last stitch of Row 4.

Join shoulders

With RS facing, slip 24 (25, 26, 27, 28, 30, 29, 31, 32, 34) held right shoulder sts to left end of needle holding left shoulder sts.

Left shoulder: (RS) K1, p1, knit to end.

Back neck: Turn work to WS and cable CO 18 (20, 20, 21, 22, 23, 29, 29, 29, 29) sts.

Right shoulder: Turn work to RS. Slip last st cast on back to LH needle, k2tog with first right shoulder st, knit to last 2 sts, p1, k1—65 (69, 71, 74, 77, 82, 86, 90, 92, 96) sts.

Next row: (WS) P1, k1, purl to last 2 sts, k1, p1.

Continue back

Row 1: (RS) K1, p1, knit to last 2 sts, p1, k1.

Row 2: P1, k1, purl to last 2 sts, k1, p1.

Rep Rows 1 and 2 until 40 (42, 42, 40, 38, 42, 42, 44, 42, 44) rows have been worked from yarn marker.

Piece should measure approx 5½ (5¾, 5¾, 5½, 5¼, 5¾, 5¾, 6, 5¾, 6)" [13.5 (14.5, 14.5, 13.5, 13, 14.5, 14.5, 15, 14.5, 15) cm] from cast-on to bottom, measured at armhole edge.

Shape underarms

While shaping the underarms, single columns of purl stitches are established on each side of the back, creating faux 'seams' defining the side panels of the sweater. These faux seams will be worked all the way to the hem.

Row 1 *inc row:* (RS) K1, p1, m1p, **pm**, knit to last 2 sts, **pm**, m1p, p1, k1—67 (71, 73, 76, 79, 84, 88, 92, 94, 98) sts.

Row 2: P1, k2, **sl m**, purl to marker, **sl m**, k2, p1.

Row 3 *inc row:* K1, p1, m1, p1, **sl m**, knit to marker, **sl m**, p1, m1, p1, k1—69 (73, 75, 78, 81, 86, 90, 94, 96, 100) sts.

Row 4: [P1, k1] twice, **sl m**, purl to marker, **sl m**, [k1, p1] twice.

Row 5 *inc row:* K1, p1, k1, LLI, p1, **sl m**, knit to marker, **sl m**, p1, RLI, k1, p1, k1—71 (75, 77, 80, 83, 88, 92, 96, 98, 102) sts.

Row 6: P1, k1, p2, k1, **sl m**, purl to marker, **sl m**, k1, p2, k1, p1.

Row 7 *inc row:* K1, p1, k1, LLI, knit to 1 st before marker, p1, **sl m**, knit to marker, **sl m**, p1, knit to last 3 sts, RLI, k1, p1, k1—2 sts increased.

neater slip-slip-knits

If your ssks look sloppier than your k2togs, try pre-turning the stitches so that the decreases can be worked with less manipulation of the fabric.

To do this, wrap the yarn back-to-front over the needle, rather than front-to-back. (It helps to watch what you normally do, then do the opposite.) This will mount the stitches with their left legs forward, setting them up for knitting through the back loop without the need to turn them before working.

Begin by wrapping the yarn backward around the needle when you work the two stitches that will be used for the decrease. As you encounter these stitches on subsequent rows, continue to wrap the yarn back-to-

front, and work the stitches through the back loop to avoid twisting. When the decreases are complete, the stitches can be worked conventionally.

Row 8: P1, k1, purl to 1 st before marker, k1, **sl m**, purl to marker, **sl m**, k1, purl to last 2 sts, k1, p1.

Rep the last two rows 2 (2, 3, 5, 7, 7, 8, 7, 10, 10) more times—77 (81, 85, 92, 99, 104, 110, 112, 120, 124) sts.

Sizes 30¾ and 32½" [78 and 83 cm]: skip to 'All sizes'
Sizes 35¾ to 55" [90.5 to 139.5 cm] only:
Next row: (RS) Cable CO – (–, 2, 2, 3, 3, 3, 3, 3, 3) sts, knit to end— – (–, 87, 94, 102, 107, 113, 115, 123, 127) sts.

Next row: Cable CO – (–, 2, 2, 3, 3, 3, 3, 3, 3) sts, purl to end— – (–, 89, 96, 105, 110, 116, 118, 126, 130) sts.

Sizes 35¾ to 45¾" [90.5 to 116 cm]: skip to 'All sizes'
Sizes 48¾ to 55" [124 to 139.5 cm] only:
Next row: (RS) Cable CO – (–, –, –, –, –, –, 3, 3, 4) sts, knit to end— – (–, –, –, –, –, –, 121, 129, 134) sts.

Next row: Cable CO – (–, –, –, –, –, –, 3, 3, 4) sts, purl to end— – (–, –, –, –, –, –, 124, 132, 138) sts.

All sizes
Piece should measure approx 7 (7¼, 7¾, 8, 8¼, 8¾, 9, 9¼, 9¾, 10)" [17.5 (18, 19.5, 20, 20.5, 22, 22.5, 23, 24.5, 25) cm] from cast-on to bottom, measured at armhole edge.

Break yarn and slip stitches onto waste yarn.

NECKBAND

With US 7 [4.5 mm] dpns and contrasting waste yarn, provisionally CO 24 sts. Change to working yarn.

Row 1: (RS) Knit.

Row 2: P1, k3, p2, [k2, p2] three times, k3, p3.

Row 3: K1, sl 1, k1, p3, k2, [p2, k2] three times, p3, k1 (selvedge stitch).

Row 4: P1, k3, p2, [k2, p2] three times, k3, sl 1 wyif, p1, sl 1 wyif.

Rep the last two rows 1 (1, 2, 2, 3, 3, 5, 5, 5, 5) more times.

Left band

Begin working left band pattern, keeping selvedge st in stockinette. Chart can be found on page 86, written instructions on page 87. Work through Row 19 of pattern.

Place back piece on flat surface. Matching cast-on edge of band to center back neck, align edge of band to left neckline and check that band is approximately 1 row shorter than length of left neckline. Slight differences can be eased in later, but if necessary, adjust length of band by adding and subtracting pairs of rows. End having worked a RS row.

Next row: Bind off 1, work next row of patt to end—23 sts.

Break yarn, leaving stitches on dpn.

Right band set-up

Carefully undo provisional CO and place 23 live stitches on an empty dpn. Mark the edge of this first row with removable stitch marker.

With RS facing, attach yarn and work as follows:

Set-up row *inc row:* (RS) K1 (selvedge stitch), p3, k2, [p2, k2] three times, p1, m1p, p1, k1, sl 1, k1—24 sts.

Row 1: (WS) Sl 1 wyif, p1, sl 1 wyif, k3, p2, [k2, p2] three times, k3, p1.

Row 2: K1, p3, k2, [p2, k2] three times, p3, k1, sl 1, k1.

Rep these two rows 1 (1, 2, 2, 3, 3, 5, 5, 5, 5) more times, then work Row 1 once more.

Right band

Begin working right band pattern, keeping selvedge stitch in stockinette. Work all 20 rows of pattern. (If you adjusted the length of the left band, make the same adjustment here.) After last row, turn work to RS. Slip 2 stitches to RH needle, pass selvedge stitch over next stitch to bind off. Slip stitch back to LH needle. Break yarn—23 sts.

FRONTS

Pick up for right front shoulder

With RS of back facing, attach yarn at right shoulder.

Set-up Row 1: (RS) *Being careful to begin with the first CO stitch*, pick up and knit 17 (18, 19, 20, 21, 23, 22, 24, 25, 27) sts. Don't pick up the final stitch, it will become a selvedge stitch. **Pm**, then work next row of right band pattern across 23 held right band sts—40 (41, 42, 43, 44, 46, 45, 47, 48, 50) sts.

Set-up Row 2: Work next row of band, purl to last 2 sts, k1, p1.

Set-up Row 3: K1, p1, knit to marker, **sl m**, work next row of band.

Shape right shoulder

Short Row 1: (WS) Work next row of band, **sl m**, p3 (4, 4, 4, 4, 5, 5, 6, 5, 6), w&t; (RS) knit to marker, **sl m**, work band sts to end.

Short Row 2: (WS) Work band sts, **sl m**, purl to wrapped st, pick up wrap, p4 (4, 4, 4, 5, 5, 5, 5, 6, 6), w&t; (RS) knit to marker, **sl m**, work band sts to end.

Short Row 3: Rep Short Row 2.

Row 4: Work band sts, **sl m**, purl to wrapped st, pick up wrap, purl to last 2 sts, k1, p1.

Tie a yarn marker around the last stitch of Row 4.

Maintaining purled 'gutter' at the right edge of piece, work even as established until 40 (42, 42, 40, 38, 42, 42, 44, 42, 44) rows have been worked from yarn marker. End having worked a WS row.

Front should measure approx 5½ (5¾, 5¾, 5½, 5¼, 5¾, 5¾, 6, 5¾, 6)" [13.5 (14.5, 14.5, 13.5, 13, 14.5, 14.5, 15, 14.5, 15) cm] from shoulder seam to bottom, measured at armhole edge.

Shape right underarm

Establish faux seam stitch as for the back.

Row 1 *inc row:* (RS) K1, p1, m1p, **pm**, work in patt to end—41 (42, 43, 44, 45, 47, 46, 48, 49, 51) sts.

Row 2: Work in patt to second marker, **sl m**, k2, p1.

Row 3 *inc row:* K1, p1, m1, p1, **sl m**, work in patt to end—42 (43, 44, 45, 46, 48, 47, 49, 50, 52) sts.

Row 4: Work in patt to second marker, **sl m**, [k1, p1] twice.

Row 5 *inc row:* K1, p1, k1, LLI, p1, **sl m**, work in patt to end—43 (44, 45, 46, 47, 49, 48, 50, 51, 53) sts.

Row 6: Work in patt to second marker, **sl m**, k1, p2, k1, p1.

Row 7 *inc row:* K1, p1, k1, LLI, knit to 1 st before marker, p1, **sl m**, work in patt to end—1 st increased.

Row 8: Work in est patts.

Rep the last two rows 2 (2, 3, 5, 7, 7, 8, 7, 10, 10) more times—46 (47, 49, 52, 55, 57, 57, 58, 62, 64) sts.

Sizes 30¾ and 32½" [78 and 83 cm]: skip to 'All sizes'
Sizes 35¾ to 55" [90.5 to 139.5 cm] only:

Next row: (RS) Cable CO – (–, 2, 2, 3, 3, 3, 3, 3, 3) sts, work in est patts to end— – (–, 51, 54, 58, 60, 60, 61, 65, 67) sts.

Next row: Work even in est patts.

Sizes 35¾ to 45¾" [90.5 to 116 cm]: skip to 'All sizes'
Sizes 48¾ to 55" [124 to 139.5 cm] only:

Next row: (RS) Cable CO – (–, –, –, –, –, –, 3, 3, 4) sts, work in est patts to end— – (–, –, –, –, –, –, 64, 68, 71) sts.

Next row: Work even in est patts.

All sizes

Front should measure approx 7 (7¼, 7¾, 8, 8¼, 8¾, 9, 9¼, 9¾, 10)" [17.5 (18, 19.5, 20, 20.5, 22, 22.5, 23, 24.5, 25) cm] from shoulder seam to bottom, measured at armhole edge.

Break yarn and slip stitches onto waste yarn.

keeping the edging smooth

Because the I-cord edging along the front bands is created with slipped stitches, its row gauge will be slightly shorter than the rest of the garment. To keep the edge from drawing up, begin working short-row I-cord segments once the fronts have been joined to the back. Work extra segments after each 20-row repeat of the band patterns as follows:

Short Row 1: (RS) K1, sl 1, k1, p1, w&t; (WS) k1, sl 1 wyif, p1, sl 1 wyif.

Next row: Work in patt to wrapped st, pick up wrap, work in patt to end.

Short Row 3: (WS) Sl 1 wyif, p1, sl 1 wyif, k1, w&t; (RS) p1, k1, sl 1, k1.

Next row: Work in patt to wrapped st, pick up wrap, work in patt to end.

Front should measure approx 5½ (5¾, 5¾, 5½, 5¼, 5¾, 5¾, 6, 5¾, 6)" [13.5 (14.5, 14.5, 13.5, 13, 14.5, 14.5, 15, 14.5, 15) cm] from shoulder seam to bottom, measured at armhole edge.

Shape left underarm

Establish faux seam stitch as for the back.

Row 1 *inc row:* (RS) Work in patt to last 2 sts, **pm**, m1p, p1, k1—41 (42, 43, 44, 45, 47, 46, 48, 49, 51) sts.

Row 2: P1, k2, **sl m**, work in patt to end.

Row 3 *inc row:* Work in patt to marker, **sl m**, p1, m1, p1, k1—42 (43, 44, 45, 46, 48, 47, 49, 50, 52) sts.

Row 4: [P1, k1] twice, **sl m**, work in patt to end.

Row 5 *inc row:* Work in patt to marker, **sl m**, p1, RLI, k1, p1, k1—43 (44, 45, 46, 47, 49, 48, 50, 51, 53) sts.

Row 6: P1, k1, p2, k1, **sl m**, work in patt to end.

Row 7 *inc row:* Work in patt to marker, **sl m**, p1, knit to last 3 sts, RLI, k1, p1, k1—1 st increased.

Row 8: Work in est patts.

Rep the last two rows 2 (2, 3, 5, 7, 7, 8, 7, 10, 10) more times—46 (47, 49, 52, 55, 57, 57, 58, 62, 64) sts.

Sizes 30¾ and 32½" [78 and 83 cm]: skip to 'All sizes'
Sizes 35¾ to 55" [90.5 to 139.5 cm] only:

Next row: (RS) Work even in est patts.

Next row: Cable CO – (–, 2, 2, 3, 3, 3, 3, 3, 3) sts, work in est patts to end— – (–, 51, 54, 58, 60, 60, 61, 65, 67) sts.

Sizes 35¾ to 45¾" [90.5 to 116 cm]: skip to 'All sizes'
Sizes 48¾ to 55" [124 to 139.5 cm] only:

Next row: (RS) Work even in est patts.

Next row: Cable CO – (–, –, –, –, –, –, 3, 3, 4) sts, work in est patts to end— – (–, –, –, –, –, –, 64, 68, 71) sts.

Pick up for left front shoulder

With RS of neckband facing, attach yarn at neck edge.

Set-up Row 1: (RS) Work next row of left band pattern, **pm**, then with RS of left shoulder facing, *skipping the first available stitch*, pick up and knit 17 (18, 19, 20, 21, 23, 22, 24, 25, 27) sts—40 (41, 42, 43, 44, 46, 45, 47, 48, 50) sts.

Set-up Row 2: P1, k1, purl to marker, **sl m**, work next row of band.

Shape left shoulder

Short Row 1: (RS) Work next row of band, **sl m**, k3 (4, 4, 4, 4, 5, 5, 6, 5, 6), w&t; (WS) purl to marker, work next row of band.

Short Row 2: (RS) Work next row of band, **sl m**, knit to wrapped st, pick up wrap, k4 (4, 4, 4, 5, 5, 5, 5, 6, 6), w&t; (WS) purl to marker, work next row of band.

Short Row 3: Rep Short Row 2.

Row 4: Work next row of band, **sl m**, knit to wrapped st, pick up wrap, knit to last 2 sts, p1, k1.

Row 5: P1, k1, purl to marker, work next row of band.

Tie a yarn marker around the last stitch of Row 5.

Maintaining purled 'gutter' at the left edge of the piece, work even est patts until 40 (42, 42, 40, 38, 42, 42, 44, 42, 44) rows have been worked from yarn marker. End having worked a WS row.

All sizes

Front should measure approx 7 (7¼, 7¾, 8, 8¼, 8¾, 9, 9¼, 9¾, 10)" [17.5 (18, 19.5, 20, 20.5, 22, 22.5, 23, 24.5, 25) cm] from shoulder seam to bottom, measured at armhole edge.

Join fronts to back

With RS facing, slip 77 (81, 89, 96, 105, 110, 116, 124, 132, 138) held back sts to left end of needle holding left front, then slip 46 (47, 51, 54, 58, 60, 60, 64, 68, 71) held right front sts to needle.

Left Front: (RS) Work next row of left band, **sl m**, work as est to end. Turn work to WS and cable CO 5 (7, 7, 7, 7, 9, 11, 11, 11, 13) sts.

Back: Turn work to RS. Slip last st cast on back to LH needle, k2tog with first back st, work in est patts to end. Turn work to WS and cable CO 5 (7, 7, 7, 7, 9, 11, 11, 11, 13) sts.

Right Front: Turn work to RS. Slip last st cast on back to LH needle, k2tog with first right front st, work as est to final marker, **sl m**, work next row of right band—177 (187, 203, 216, 233, 246, 256, 272, 288, 304) sts.

Next row: Work right band, **sl m**, work as established to final marker, **sl m**, work left band.

BODICE

From here to the hem, regular increases will be made to the fronts every 10 rows, beginning with the next RS row.

Next row *front inc row:* (RS) Work in patt to first marker, **sl m**, k2, RLI, work in patt to 2 sts before final marker, LLI, k2, **sl m**, work in patt to end—2 sts increased to fronts.

Continue as established, working band patterns at each front edge, faux seam stitches at the side panels,

and front increases every 10th row, until bodice is approx ½ to 1" [1.5 to 2.5 cm] below apex of bust. End having worked a WS row.

Begin underbust decreases

Next row *dec row:* (RS) * Work in patt to first underarm marker, **sl m**, p1, k1, ssk, knit to 4 sts before next underarm marker, k2tog, k1, p1, **sl m**; rep from * once more, work in patt to end—4 sts decreased.

Next 5 rows: Work even in est patts.

Rep these six rows three more times—total of 16 sts decreased at underbust.

Continue in est patts until bodice is approx ¾ to 1" [2 to 2.5 cm] above waistline or narrowest part of torso. End having worked a WS row.

Begin hip increases

Next row *inc row:* (RS) * Work in patt to first underarm marker, **sl m**, p1, k2, RLI, knit to 3 sts before next underarm marker, LLI, k2, p1, **sl m**; rep from * once more, work in patt to end—4 sts increased.

Next 5 rows: Work even in est patts.

Rep these six rows five more times—total of 24 sts increased for hips.

Work even in est patts until sweater measures 21⅞ (22⅝, 23⅛, 23⅞, 24⅛, 25⅛, 25⅜, 26⅛, 26⅝, 27⅜)" [55.5 (57.5, 58.5, 60.5, 61.5, 64, 64.5, 66.5, 67.5, 69.5) cm] from neck edge of shoulder to bottom, or desired length, less ⅜" [1 cm]. End having worked either Row 7, 15, 17, or 19 of band patterns—207 (217, 233, 248, 265, 278, 288, 306, 322, 338) sts.

Last row: (WS) Work in est patts to last 23 sts. Place 23 left band sts on holder. Turn work.

mind the gauge

Many knitters have a slightly different tension depending on whether they are knitting flat or knitting in the round. But did you know that your in-the-round gauge can also change depending on the circumference of the item you are knitting? Frequently, a knitter's stitch gauge will be a little bit tighter around a small circumference. This can lead to sleeves that fit a bit more snugly than you may have intended.

Take note of whether your gauge becomes tighter when working a sleeve in the round. If it does, consider going up a needle size after working the sleeve cap—or adjust the number and rate of sleeve decreases to maintain the desired fit.

I-cord bind-off

Change to US 4 [3.25 mm] circ.

Bind-off row: (RS) CO 3 sts to LH needle using the knitted cast-on method. K2, k2tog-tbl with st from body, * sl 3 sts back to LH needle, pull yarn firmly across back of work, k2, k2tog-tbl; rep from * until 1 body st remains before right band sts. Sl 3 sts back to LH needle, k2tog, k2tog-tbl. Bind off 2 remaining sts.

Right band

Work right band finishing rows to shape bottom of band (see page 86 for chart, page 87 for written instructions). Bind off all sts loosely in pattern.

sleeves and fit

When the sleeves go onto a sweater, it affects the overall shape of the garment. The weight of the sleeves plus the width of your shoulders will tend to broaden the upper bodice slightly, stretching the fabric width-wise. Adding sleeves also raises the bottoms of the armholes, as the previously unsupported fabric is shaped to the sleeve cap. In compensation, the garment will become slightly shorter. If the bust or hips are intended to fit with negative ease, this can shorten it further still.

It's a lot easier to judge the final length of the garment when the sleeves are in place. If you'd like a more accurate idea of how your sweater will ultimately fit, feel free to skip ahead and knit the sleeves before completing the body.

Once you've worked the body for a least a couple of inches below the armholes, just slip the body stitches onto waste yarn and proceed with the sleeves. After they are finished, resume knitting the body. When deciding on a final length for your sweater, remember to factor in any changes that you saw in your swatch after washing and blocking it.

Left band

With WS facing, attach yarn and work left band finishing rows to shape bottom of band. Bind off all stitches loosely in pattern. Thread tail onto needle and seam edge of band to I-cord.

Seam neckband

Using locking stitch markers, match center back neck of sweater with center of neckband, then clip neckband to sweater in several more places, easing fabric at the curves.

Thread yarn needle with a length of yarn at least four times as wide as neck opening. Starting at the first cast-on stitch at the right side of the neck, begin seaming using mattress stitch. Leave a long enough tail to be able to complete the seam to the right shoulder later.

On the body side of work, pass needle under both legs of each stitch. On the neckband side, pass needle under one purl bump. As needed, pick up two purl bumps on neckband to match the stitch gauge of the body.

Where neck curves and stitches are to be joined vertically, begin picking up the horizontal bar between stitches on the body, and continue going under a single purl bump on the neckband.

SLEEVES

Note: Pick up stitches using smaller gauge needle, then transfer them to 16" [40 cm] long US 7 [4.5 mm] circ before beginning to work sleeve cap.

Place a removable stitch marker on front and back 1⅛ (1¼, 1¼, 1⅜, 1½, 1⅝, 1¾, 1⅞, 2, 2⅛)" [2.75 (3, 3.25, 3.5, 3.75, 4.25, 4.5, 4.75, 5, 5.25) cm] away from the shoulder seam. Place a third marker at the center of the underarm. The marker to right of shoulder seam is **M-one**, to left of shoulder is **M-two**, at underarm is **M-three**.

Begin at **M-one**. Working just inside the column of knit sts on the edge of armhole, pick up and knit 14 (15, 15, 18, 20, 22, 24, 26, 28, 28) sts between **M-one**

and **M-two**, pick up and knit 25 (26, 26, 27, 27, 29, 29, 29, 30, 31) sts between **M-two** and the cast-on sts at underarm, **pm**, pick up and knit 1 st in each of the 2 (3, 5, 5, 6, 7, 8, 11, 11, 13) cast-on sts before **M-three**, place unique marker for beginning of round, pick up and knit 1 st in each of the remaining 2 (3, 5, 5, 6, 7, 8, 11, 11, 13) cast-on sts at underarm, **pm**, pick up and knit 25 (26, 26, 27, 27, 29, 29, 29, 30, 31) more sts, ending at **M-one**—68 (73, 77, 82, 86, 94, 98, 106, 110, 116) sts.

Remove **M-one**, **M-two** and **M-three**.

Shape upper cap

When working the short rows that shape the sleeve caps, the wraps are not picked up; they are left in place and the wrapped stitch is worked in the normal fashion.

Short Row 1: (RS) K14 (15, 15, 18, 20, 22, 24, 26, 28, 28), w&t; (WS) p14 (15, 15, 18, 20, 22, 24, 26, 28, 28), w&t.

Short Row 2: (RS) Knit to prev wrapped st, knit wrapped st, sl 1 wyif, shift yarn to back, w&t; (WS) purl to prev wrapped st, purl wrapped st, sl 1 wyib, bring yarn to front, w&t.

Rep Short Row 2 twice more.

Shape mid cap

Next short row: (RS) Knit to prev wrapped st, knit wrapped st, w&t; (WS) purl to prev wrapped st, purl wrapped st, w&t.

Rep this row, working back and forth to build the sleeve cap, until 5 sts remain before each of the side markers that separate the underarm sts from the sleeve cap.

Work sleeve in the round

Rnd 1 *dec rnd:* K1 (2, 4, 4, 5, 6, 7, 10, 10, 12), k2tog with remaining wrapped st, knit to end of round—62 (67, 71, 76, 80, 88, 92, 100, 104, 110) sts.

Next 6 rnds: Knit.

Change to preferred needle style for small circumference knitting in the round when necessary.

Next rnd *dec rnd:* K1, ssk, knit to last 3 sts, k2tog, k1—2 sts decreased.

Work *dec rnd* every 13th (12th, 9th, 8th, 6th, 5th, 5th, 6th, 5th, 4th) rnd 2 (2, 3, 3, 4, 5, 5, 4, 5, 6) more times, then every 16th (12th, 10th, 10th, 10th, 7th, 7th, 5th, 5th, 5th) rnd 4 (6, 7, 8, 8, 11, 11, 16, 16, 18) more times—48 (49, 49, 52, 54, 54, 58, 58, 60, 60) sts.

Work even until sleeve measures approx 16⅛ (16⅝, 16⅝, 17⅛, 17⅛, 17⅝, 17⅝, 18⅛, 18⅛, 18⅝)" [41 (42, 42, 43.5, 43.5, 45, 45, 46, 46, 47.5) cm] from underarm, or desired sleeve length, less ⅜" [1 cm].

Change to US 4 [3.5 mm] needle, and work I-cord bind off as for hem. Break yarn, thread tail onto yarn needle, and sew ends of I-cord edging together.

FINISHING

Weave in all ends. Block sweater to measurements.

Shape lower cap

Next short row: (RS) Knit to prev wrapped st, knit wrapped st, then wrap the next 2 sts together & turn; (WS) purl to prev wrapped st, purl wrapped st, then wrap the next 2 sts together & turn.

Next short row *dec row:* (RS) Knit to twin-wrapped sts, knit wrapped sts tog as one st, wrap 2 sts together & turn; (WS) purl to twin-wrapped sts, purl wrapped sts tog as one st, wrap 2 sts together & turn—2 sts decreased.

Rep this row until 1 st remains before each side marker.

Next short row *dec row:* (RS) Knit to twin-wrapped sts, knit wrapped sts tog as one st, wrap next *single* st, remove marker & turn; (WS) purl to twin-wrapped sts, purl wrapped sts tog as one st, wrap next *single* st, remove marker & turn—64 (69, 73, 78, 82, 90, 94, 102, 106, 112) sts.

Last row *dec row:* (RS) Knit to prev wrapped st, k2tog-tbl with next st, k1 (2, 4, 4, 5, 6, 7, 10, 10, 12)—63 (68, 72, 77, 81, 89, 93, 101, 105, 111) sts.

Left band

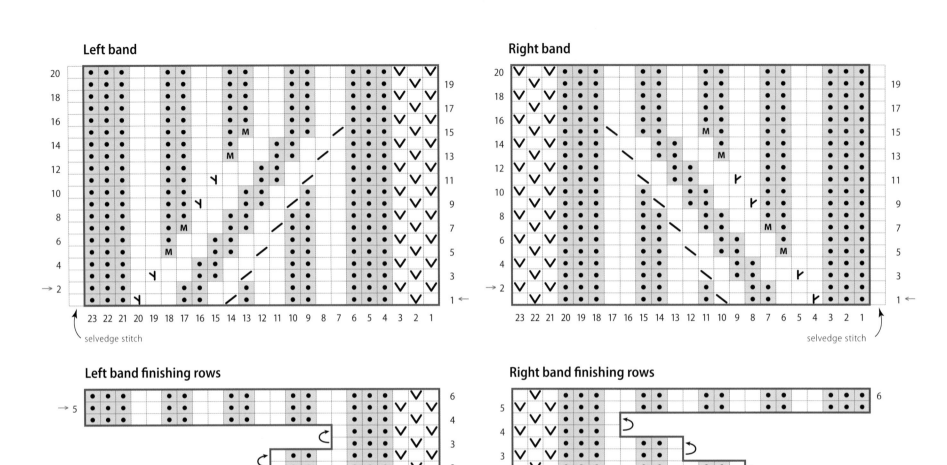

Right band

selvedge stitch

selvedge stitch

Left band finishing rows

Right band finishing rows

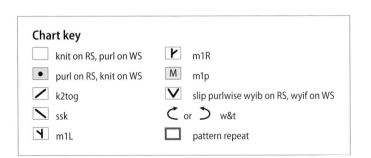

Chart key

☐	knit on RS, purl on WS	⊬	m1R
•	purl on RS, knit on WS	M	m1p
╱	k2tog	V	slip purlwise wyib on RS, wyif on WS
╲	ssk	↻ or ↺	w&t
⅄	m1L	☐	pattern repeat

If the ssks on the right band look a little wobbly, try the technique described in *'Neater slip-slip-knits'*, page 80.

line-by-line instructions for edging patterns

Left band

Row 1: (RS) K1, sl 1, k1, p3, k2, p2, k2, p1, k2tog, k1, p2, k2, m1L, p3.

Row 2: K3, p3, k2, p2, k1, p2, k2, p2, k3, sl 1 wyif, p1, sl 1 wyif.

Row 3: K1, sl 1, k1, p3, k2, p2, k2, k2tog, k1, p2, k2, m1L, k1, p3.

Row 4: K3, [p4, k2] twice, p2, k3, sl 1 wyif, p1, sl 1 wyif.

Row 5: K1, sl 1, k1, p3, k2, p2, k1, k2tog, k1, p2, k2, m1p, k2, p3.

Row 6: K3, p2, k1, p2, k2, p3, k2, p2, k3, sl 1 wyif, p1, sl 1 wyif.

Row 7: K1, sl 1, k1, p3, k2, p2, k2tog, k1, p2, k2, m1p, p1, k2, p3.

Row 8: K3, [p2, k2] three times, p2, k3, sl 1 wyif, p1, sl 1 wyif.

Row 9: K1, sl 1, k1, p3, k2, p1, k2tog, k1, p2, k2, m1L, p2, k2, p3.

Row 10: K3, p2, k2, p3, k2, p2, k1, p2, k3, sl 1 wyif, p1, sl 1 wyif.

Row 11: K1, sl 1, k1, p3, k2, k2tog, k1, p2, k2, m1L, k1, p2, k2, p3.

Row 12: K3, p2, [k2, p4] twice, k3, sl 1 wyif, p1, sl 1 wyif.

Row 13: K1, sl 1, k1, p3, k1, k2tog, k1, p2, k2, m1p, k2, p2, k2, p3.

Row 14: K3, p2, k2, p2, k1, p2, k2, p3, k3, sl 1 wyif, p1, sl 1 wyif.

Row 15: K1, sl 1, k1, p3, k2tog, k1, p2, k2, m1p, p1, k2, p2, k2, p3.

Row 16: K3, [p2, k2] three times, p2, k3, sl 1 wyif, p1, sl 1 wyif.

Row 17: K1, sl 1, k1, p3, [k2, p2] three times, k2, p3.

Row 18: Rep Row 16.

Row 19: Rep Row 17.

Row 20: Rep Row 16.

Right band

Row 1: (RS) P3, m1R, k2, p2, k1, ssk, p1, k2, p2, k2, p3, k1, sl 1, k1.

Row 2: Sl 1 wyif, p1, sl 1 wyif, k3, p2, k2, p2, k1, p2, k2, p3, k3.

Row 3: P3, k1, m1R, k2, p2, k1, ssk, k2, p2, k2, p3, k1, sl 1, k1.

Row 4: Sl 1 wyif, p1, sl 1 wyif, k3, p2, [k2, p4] twice, k3.

Row 5: P3, k2, m1p, k2, p2, k1, ssk, k1, p2, k2, p3, k1, sl 1, k1.

Row 6: Sl 1 wyif, p1, sl 1 wyif, k3, p2, k2, p3, k2, p2, k1, p2, k3.

Row 7: P3, k2, p1, m1p, k2, p2, k1, ssk, p2, k2, p3, k1, sl 1, k1.

Row 8: Sl 1 wyif, p1, sl 1 wyif, k3, [p2, k2] three times, p2, k3.

Row 9: P3, k2, p2, m1R, k2, p2, k1, ssk, p1, k2, p3, k1, sl 1, k1.

Row 10: Sl 1 wyif, p1, sl 1 wyif, k3, p2, k1, p2, k2, p3, k2, p2, k3.

Row 11: P3, k2, p2, k1, m1R, k2, p2, k1, ssk, k2, p3, k1, sl 1, k1.

Row 12: Sl 1 wyif, p1, sl 1 wyif, k3, [p4, k2] twice, p2, k3.

Row 13: P3, k2, p2, k2, m1p, k2, p2, k1, ssk, k1, p3, k1, sl 1, k1.

Row 14: Sl 1 wyif, p1, sl 1 wyif, k3, p3, k2, p2, k1, p2, k2, p2, k3.

Row 15: P3, k2, p2, k2, p1, m1p, k2, p2, k1, ssk, p3, k1, sl 1, k1.

Row 16: Sl 1 wyif, p1, sl 1 wyif, k3, [p2, k2] three times, p2, k3.

Row 17: P3, [k2, p2] three times, k2, p3, k1, sl 1, k1.

Row 18: Rep Row 16.

Row 19: Rep Row 17.

Row 20: Rep Row 16.

Left band finishing rows

Short Row 1: (RS) K1, sl 1, k1, p3, [k2, p2] twice, k1, w&t; (WS) p1, [k2, p2] twice, k3, sl 1 wyif, p1, sl 1 wyif.

Short Row 2: (RS) K1, sl 1, k1, p3, k2, p2, k1, w&t; (WS) p1, k2, p2, k3, sl 1 wyif, p1, sl 1 wyif.

Short Row 3: (RS) K1, sl 1, k1, p3, k1, w&t; (WS) p1, k3, sl 1 wyif, p1, sl 1 wyif.

Row 4: Picking up wraps as you come to them, k1, sl 1, k1, p3, [k2, p2] three times, k2, p3.

Row 5: K3, [p2, k2] three times, p2, k3, sl 1 wyif, p1, sl 1 wyif.

Row 6: K1, sl 1, k1, p3, [k2, p2] three times, k2, p3.

Right band finishing rows

Row 1: (RS) P3, [k2, p2] three times, k2, p3, k1, sl 1, k1.

Short Row 2: (WS) Sl 1 wyif, p1, sl 1 wyif, k3, [p2, k2] twice, p1, w&t; (RS) k1, [p2, k2] twice, p3, k1, sl 1, k1.

Short Row 3: (WS) Sl 1 wyif, p1, sl 1 wyif, k3, p2, k2, p1, w&t; (RS) k1, p2, k2, p3, k1, sl 1, k1.

Short Row 4: (WS) Sl 1 wyif, p1, sl 1 wyif, k3, p1, w&t; (RS) k1, p3, k1, sl 1, k1.

Row 5: Picking up wraps as you come to them, sl 1 wyif, p1, sl 1 wyif, k3, [p2, k2] three times, p2, k3.

Row 6: P3, [k2, p2] three times, k2, p3, k1, sl 1, k1.

clarendon *between spart + FW* (handwritten)

Quick and cozy, Clarendon is designed with a bit of positive ease in the body. To preserve the oversized feel while keeping a good fit in the shoulders, the armhole fronts are contoured, creating a slightly narrower cross-front width in the upper bodice. Chunky slip-stitch ribbing finishes the neck, cuffs and hem.

Finished measurements

Front shoulder width: 11½ (12½, 13, 13½, 14¼, 15¼, 15¾, 16¾, 17¼, 17¾)" [29 (32, 33, 34.5, 36, 38.5, 40, 42.5, 44, 45.5) cm]

Bust circumference: 33½ (36¾, 39, 42¼, 45¼, 48½, 51¾, 53¾, 57, 60¼)" [85.5 (93.5, 99, 107, 115, 123.5, 131.5, 137, 145, 153) cm]

Sample shown in 13½" [34.5 cm] shoulder, 42¼" [107 cm] bust size.

Suggested ease at bust: +3 to +4" [+7.5 to +10 cm]

Materials
Yarn   *Sport* (handwritten)

Osprey by Quince & Co.
(100% American wool; 170 yd [155 m] / 100 g)

• 5 (5, 6, 6, 7, 7, 8, 8, 9, 9) skeins Belize (139)

Needles

Body
• US 10.5 [6.5 mm] circ, 24" [60 cm] long
• US 10.5 [6.5 mm] circ, 32" [80 cm] long or longer

Sleeves
• US 10.5 [6.5 mm] circ, 16" [40 cm] long
• US 10.5 [6.5 mm] needles of preferred style for working small circumferences in the round
• US 10 [6 mm] needles of preferred style for working small circumferences in the round
• US 9 [5.5 mm] needles of preferred style for working small circumferences in the round

Neckband
• US 8 [5 mm] circ, 24" [60 cm] long

Or size to obtain gauge

Optional
• Extra US 6 [4 mm] circ to facilitate trying on garment

Notions
• Waste yarn of similar gauge and contrasting color
• Stitch markers, both removable and fixed ring, including one unique for beginning of round
• Yarn needle

Gauge
15 sts and 23 rows/rnds = 4" [10 cm] in stockinette stitch, on US 10.5 [6.5 mm] needles, after blocking.

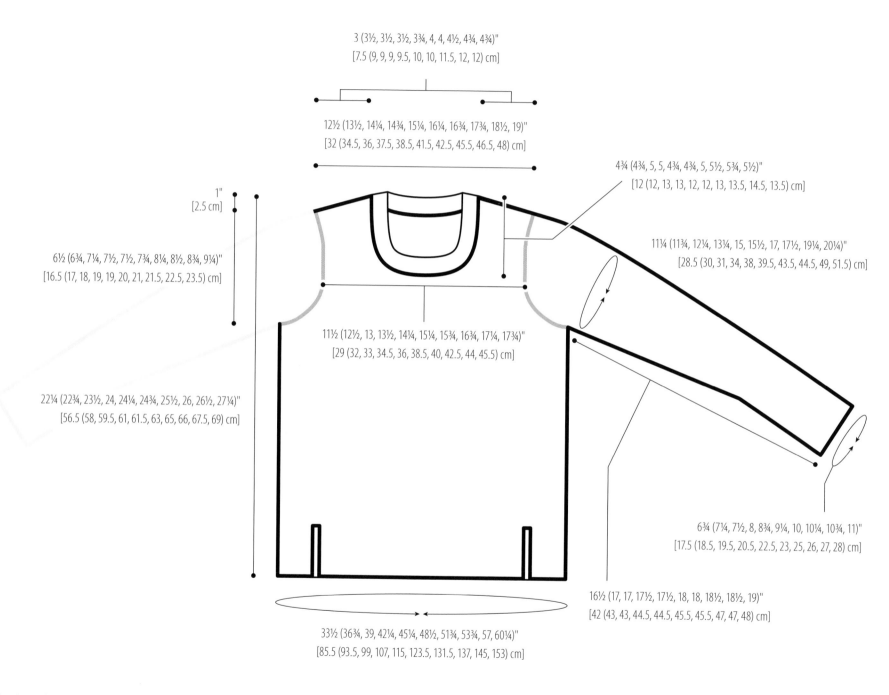

3 (3½, 3½, 3½, 3¾, 4, 4, 4½, 4¾, 4¾)"
[7.5 (9, 9, 9, 9.5, 10, 10, 11.5, 12, 12) cm]

12½ (13½, 14¼, 14¾, 15¼, 16¼, 16¾, 17¾, 18½, 19)"
[32 (34.5, 36, 37.5, 38.5, 41.5, 42.5, 45.5, 46.5, 48) cm]

4¾ (4¾, 5, 5, 4¾, 4¾, 5, 5½, 5¾, 5½)"
[12 (12, 13, 13, 12, 12, 13, 13.5, 14.5, 13.5) cm]

1"
[2.5 cm]

11¼ (11¾, 12¼, 13¼, 15, 15½, 17, 17½, 19¼, 20¼)"
[28.5 (30, 31, 34, 38, 39.5, 43.5, 44.5, 49, 51.5) cm]

6½ (6¾, 7¼, 7½, 7½, 7¾, 8¼, 8½, 8¾, 9¼)"
[16.5 (17, 18, 19, 19, 20, 21, 21.5, 22.5, 23.5) cm]

11½ (12½, 13, 13½, 14¼, 15¼, 15¾, 16¾, 17¼, 17¾)"
[29 (32, 33, 34.5, 36, 38.5, 40, 42.5, 44, 45.5) cm]

22¼ (22¾, 23½, 24, 24¼, 24¾, 25½, 26, 26½, 27¼)"
[56.5 (58, 59.5, 61, 61.5, 63, 65, 66, 67.5, 69) cm]

6¾ (7¼, 7½, 8, 8¾, 9¼, 10, 10¼, 10¾, 11)"
[17.5 (18.5, 19.5, 20.5, 22.5, 23, 25, 26, 27, 28) cm]

16½ (17, 17, 17½, 17½, 18, 18, 18½, 18½, 19)"
[42 (43, 43, 44.5, 44.5, 45.5, 45.5, 47, 47, 48) cm]

33½ (36¾, 39, 42¼, 45¼, 48½, 51¾, 53¾, 57, 60¼)"
[85.5 (93.5, 99, 107, 115, 123.5, 131.5, 137, 145, 153) cm]

BACK (begin at back shoulders)

With shorter US 10.5 [6.5 mm] circ and the long-tail cast-on, loosely CO 49 (53, 55, 57, 59, 63, 65, 69, 71, 73) sts. Clip a locking stitch marker to cast-on edge (not over the needle), 13 (15, 15, 15, 16, 17, 17, 19, 20, 20) sts from each end of needle.

Shape right shoulder and neck

Short Row 1: (WS) P1, k1, p11 (13, 13, 13, 14, 15, 15, 17, 18, 18), w&t; (RS) k3 (3, 3, 3, 3, 4, 4, 4, 4, 4), w&t.

Short Row 2: (WS) Purl to prev wrap, pick up wrap, w&t; (RS) knit to prev wrap, pick up wrap, k2 (3, 3, 3, 3, 3, 4, 4, 4), w&t.

Short Row 3: Rep Short Row 2.

Short Row 4: (WS) Purl to prev wrap, pick up wrap, p1, w&t; (RS) knit to last 2 sts, picking up prev wrap, p1, k1.

Shape left shoulder and neck

Short Row 1: (WS) P1, k1, purl to prev wrap, pick up wrap, purl to last 10 (12, 12, 12, 13, 14, 13, 15, 16, 16) sts, w&t; (RS) k3 (3, 3, 3, 3, 4, 4, 4, 4, 4), w&t.

Short Row 2: (WS) Purl to prev wrap, pick up wrap, p2 (3, 3, 3, 3, 3, 4, 4, 4), w&t; (RS) knit to prev wrap, pick up wrap, w&t.

Short Row 3: Rep Short Row 2.

Short Row 4: (WS) Purl to last 2 sts, picking up prev wrap, k1, p1, turn work; (RS) knit to prev wrap, pick up wrap, k1, w&t.

Next row: Purl to last 2 sts, k1, p1.

Next row: K1, p1, knit to prev wrap, pick up wrap, knit to last 2 sts, p1, k1.

Next row: P1, k1, purl to last 2 sts, k1, p1.

Tie a yarn marker around the last stitch of the row just worked.

Continue upper back

Row 1: (RS) K1, p1, knit to last 2 sts, p1, k1.

Row 2: P1, k1, purl to last 2 sts, k1, p1.

Rep Rows 1 and 2 until 26 (26, 28, 28, 26, 26, 28, 30, 32, 30) rows have been worked from yarn marker. Piece should measure approx 5 (5, 5½, 5½, 5, 5, 5½, 5¾, 6, 5¾)" [13 (13, 14, 14, 13, 13, 14, 15, 15.5, 15) cm] from cast-on to bottom, measured at armhole edge.

Shape underarms

Next row *inc row:* (RS) K1, p1, k1, RLI, knit to last 3 sts, LLI, k1, p1, k1—2 sts increased.

Next row: P1, k1, purl to last 2 sts, k1, p1.

Rep these two rows 2 (3, 3, 4, 4, 5, 5, 5, 5, 7) more times—55 (61, 63, 67, 69, 75, 77, 81, 83, 89) sts.

Next row: (RS) Cable CO 2 (2, 2, 3, 2, 2, 3, 3, 3, 3) sts, knit to end—57 (63, 65, 70, 71, 77, 80, 84, 86, 92) sts.

Next row: Cable CO 2 (2, 2, 3, 2, 2, 3, 3, 3, 3) sts, purl to end—59 (65, 67, 73, 73, 79, 83, 87, 89, 95) sts.

Sizes 33½ to 42¼" [85.5 to 107 cm]: skip to 'All sizes'
Sizes 45¼ to 60¼" [115 to 153 cm] only:

Next row: (RS) Cable CO – (–, –, –, 3, 3, 3, 3, 4, 4) sts, knit to end— – (–, –, –, 76, 82, 86, 90, 93, 99) sts.

Next row: Cable CO – (–, –, –, 3, 3, 3, 3, 4, 4) sts, purl to end— – (–, –, –, 79, 85, 89, 93, 97, 103) sts.

All sizes

Piece should measure approx 6½ (6¾, 7¼, 7½, 7½, 7¾, 8¼, 8½, 8¾, 9¼)" [16.5 (17, 18, 19, 19, 20, 21, 21.5, 22.5, 23.5) cm] from cast-on to bottom, measured at armhole edge.

Break yarn and slip 59 (65, 67, 73, 79, 85, 89, 93, 97, 103) stitches onto waste yarn.

FRONTS

Left front shoulder

With RS facing, attach yarn at neck edge of left shoulder. With US 10.5 [6.5 mm] circ, pick up and knit 12 (14, 14, 14, 15, 16, 16, 18, 19, 19) stitches along cast-on edge, making sure to insert needle under both legs of each cast-on stitch.

Set-up row: (WS) P1, kfpb, purl to end—13 (15, 15, 15, 16, 17, 17, 19, 20, 20) sts.

Shape shoulder

Short Row 1: (RS) K3 (3, 3, 3, 3, 4, 4, 4, 4, 4), w&t; (WS) purl to end.

Short Row 2: (RS) Knit to prev wrap, pick up wrap, k2 (3, 3, 3, 3, 3, 4, 4, 4), w&t; (WS) purl to end.

Short Row 3: Rep Short Row 2.

Next row: (RS) Knit to prev wrap, pick up wrap, knit to last 2 sts, p1, k1.

Next row: P1, k1, purl to end.

Tie a yarn marker around the first stitch of the row just worked, at the armhole edge.

Shape upper armhole

Row 1 *dec row:* (RS) Knit to last 5 sts, k2tog, k1, p1, k1—1 st decreased.

Row 2: P1, k1, purl to end.

Rep Rows 1 and 2 once more—11 (13, 13, 13, 14, 15, 15, 17, 18, 18) sts.

Continue left front

Row 1: (RS) Knit to last 2 sts, p1, k1.

Row 2: P1, k1, purl to end.

Rep Rows 1 and 2 until 10 (10, 12, 12, 10, 10, 12, 14, 16, 14) rows have been worked from yarn marker.

Shape left neck edge

Next row *inc row:* (RS) K2, RLI, knit to last 2 sts, p1, k1—1 st increased.

Next row: Purl to last 2 sts, k1, p1.

Rep these two rows once more—13 (15, 15, 15, 16, 17, 17, 19, 20, 20) sts.

Piece should measure approx 3 (3, 3¼, 3¼, 3, 3, 3¼, 3¾, 4, 3¾)" [7.5 (7.5, 8.5, 8.5, 7.5, 7.5, 8.5, 9.5, 10, 9.5) cm] from shoulder seam to bottom, measured at armhole edge.

Break yarn and place stitches onto holder.

Right front shoulder

With RS facing, attach yarn at armhole edge of left shoulder. With US 10.5 [6.5 mm] circ, pick up and knit 12 (14, 14, 14, 15, 16, 16, 18, 19, 19) stitches along cast-on edge, making sure to insert needle under both legs of each cast-on stitch.

Set-up Row 1: (WS) Purl to last 2 sts, pfkb, p1—13 (15, 15, 15, 16, 17, 17, 19, 20, 20) sts.

Set-up Row 2: K1, p1, knit to end.

Shape shoulder

Short Row 1: (WS) P3 (3, 3, 3, 3, 4, 4, 4, 4, 4), w&t; (RS) knit to end.

Short Row 2: (WS) Purl to prev wrap, pick up wrap, p2 (3, 3, 3, 3, 3, 3, 4, 4, 4), w&t; (RS) knit to end.

Short Row 3: Rep Short Row 2.

Next row: Purl to prev wrap, pick up wrap, purl to last 2 sts, k1, p1.

Tie a yarn marker around the last stitch of the row just worked.

Shape upper armhole

Row 1 *dec row:* (RS) K1, p1, k1, ssk, knit to end—1 st decreased.

Row 2: Purl to last 2 sts, k1, p1.

Rep Rows 1 and 2 once more—11 (13, 13, 13, 14, 15, 15, 17, 18, 18) sts.

Continue right front

Row 1: (RS) K1, p1, knit to end.

Row 2: Purl to last 2 sts, k1, p1.

Rep Rows 1 and 2 until 10 (10, 12, 12, 10, 10, 12, 14, 16, 14) rows have been worked from yarn marker.

Shape right neck edge

Next row *inc row:* (RS) K1, p1, knit to last 2 sts, LLI, k2—1 st increased.

Next row: Purl to last 2 sts, k1, p1.

Rep these two rows once more—13 (15, 15, 15, 16, 17, 17, 19, 20, 20) sts.

Piece should measure approx 3 (3, 3¼, 3¼, 3, 3, 3¼, 3¾ 4, 3¾)" [7.5 (7.5, 8.5, 8.5, 7.5, 7.5, 8.5, 9.5, 10, 9.5) cm] from shoulder seam to bottom, measured at armhole edge.

Do not break yarn.

Join fronts

With RS facing, slip 13 (15, 15, 15, 16, 17, 17, 19, 20, 20) held left front sts to left end of needle holding right front sts.

Right front: (RS) K1, p1, knit to end.

Front neckline: Turn work to WS, and loosely CO 20 (20, 22, 24, 24, 26, 28, 28, 28, 30) sts, using the cable cast on.

Left shoulder: Turn work to RS. Slip last st cast on back to LH needle, k2tog with first left shoulder st, knit to last 2 sts, p1, k1—45 (49, 51, 53, 55, 59, 61, 65, 67, 69) sts.

Shape left neckline

Continuing in established patts, beginning on WS at left armhole edge, work pairs of short rows to curve and lower the neckline.

Short Row 1: (WS) P1, k1, p14 (16, 16, 16, 17, 18, 18, 20, 21, 21), w&t; (RS) knit to last 2 sts, p1, k1.

Short Row 2: (WS) P1, k1, purl to prev wrap, pick up wrap, p2 (2, 2, 3, 3, 3, 3, 4, 4, 4), w&t; (RS) knit to last 2 sts, p1, k1.

Next row: P1, k1, purl to prev wrap, pick up wrap, purl across neckline to last 2 sts, k1, p1.

a couture detail

Contoured upper armholes are a little trick I've borrowed from high-end commercial knitwear. The technique is used in Clarendon to allow the back of the sweater to be slightly wider than the front. The shaping at the shoulder nips the vertical line of the armhole in just enough for the sweater to hang properly, while preserving the garment's feeling of slightly oversized ease.

Oversized garments are not the only place where this trick comes in handy. Many of us have a cross-back measurement that's a little bit wider than the cross-front dimension. Adding upper armhole contouring to the front of a set-in sleeve sweater is an easy way to improve the fit. Likewise, an open-front cardigan will stay on the shoulders better with a small amount of front armhole shaping.

Adding upper armhole contouring to any of the designs in this book is easy. Work the upper back as directed. Once you've completed the shoulder shaping on the first front, work single decreases on the first few right side rows before continuing with the pattern directions. Work the same number of decreases for the second front. Place the decreases a few stitches in from the armhole edge (see '*Shape upper armhole*', pages 91 and 92). In stockinette fabric, use k2tog decreases on the left front, and ssk on the right.

How much shaping is needed? Very fine-gauge commercial knits can take out as much as an inch [2.5 cm] from each front armhole. But it's best to keep the shaping fairly close to the shoulder seam, so for handknits, decreasing by 2 or 3 stitches at each armhole is usually prefer-

able. That small bit of contouring will still make a big difference.

Each stitch that is decreased in the upper armhole must be added back in to the lower armhole shaping so that the final garment circumference remains the same. If, for example, you've decreased 2 stitches on each side, you'd begin the underarm increases 4 rows higher than the pattern instructions say to, allowing you to make 2 extra increases on the right side rows.

If you happened to be working a garment from the bottom up, you'd reverse the procedure, working a few extra decreases as you shape the lower armhole on each front, and making increases to get back to the specified shoulder width as you approach the top of the armhole.

Shape right neckline

Work short row pairs as for left neckline.

Short Row 1: (RS) K1, p1, k14 (16, 16, 16, 17, 18, 18, 20, 21, 21), w&t; (WS) purl to last 2 sts, k1, p1.

Short Row 2: (RS) K1, p1, knit to prev wrap, pick up wrap, k2 (2, 2, 3, 3, 3, 4, 4, 4), w&t; (WS) purl to last 2 sts, k1, p1.

Next row: K1, p1, knit to prev wrap, pick up wrap, knit to last 2 sts, p1, k1.

Next row: P1, k1, purl to last 2 sts, k1, p1.

Neckline shaping is complete. Piece should measure approx 4¼ (4¼, 4¾, 4¾, 4¼, 4¼, 4¾, 5, 5½, 5)" [11 (11, 12, 12, 11, 11, 12, 13, 13.5, 13) cm] from shoulder seam to bottom, measured at armhole edge.

Shape underarms

Next row *inc row:* (RS) K1, p1, k1, RLI, knit to last 3 sts, LLI, k1, p1, k1—2 sts increased.

Next row: P1, k1, purl to last 2 sts, k1, p1.

Rep these two rows 4 (5, 5, 6, 6, 7, 7, 7, 7, 9) more times—55 (61, 63, 67, 69, 75, 77, 81, 83, 89) sts.

Next row: (RS) Cable CO 2 (2, 2, 3, 2, 2, 3, 3, 3, 3) sts, knit to end—57 (63, 65, 70, 71, 77, 80, 84, 86, 92) sts.

Next row: Cable CO 2 (2, 2, 3, 2, 2, 3, 3, 3, 3) sts, purl to end—59 (65, 67, 73, 73, 79, 83, 87, 89, 95) sts.

Sizes 33½ to 42¼" [85.5 to 107 cm]: skip to 'All sizes'
Sizes 45¼ to 60¼" [115 to 153 cm] only:

Next row: (RS) Cable CO – (–, –, –, 3, 3, 3, 3, 4, 4) sts, knit to end— – (–, –, –, 76, 82, 86, 90, 93, 99) sts.

Next row: Cable CO – (–, –, –, 3, 3, 3, 3, 4, 4) sts, purl to end— – (–, –, –, 79, 85, 89, 93, 97, 103) sts.

All sizes
Piece should measure approx 6½ (6¾, 7¼, 7½, 7½, 7¾, 8¼, 8½, 8¾, 9¼)" [16.5 (17, 18, 19, 19, 20, 21, 21.5, 22.5, 23.5) cm] from cast-on to bottom, measured at armhole edge.

Join front to back

With RS facing, slip 59 (65, 67, 73, 79, 85, 89, 93, 97, 103) held back sts to left end of needle holding front.

Front and left underarm: (RS) Knit to end. Turn work to WS and cable CO 2 (2, 3, 3, 3, 3, 4, 4, 5, 5) sts, **pm**, cable CO 3 (3, 4, 4, 4, 4, 5, 5, 6, 6) more sts.

Back and right underarm: Turn work to RS. Slip last st cast on back to LH needle, k2tog with first back st, knit to end. Turn work to WS and cable CO 2 (2, 3, 3, 3, 4, 4, 5, 5) sts, place unique marker for beginning of round, cable CO 3 (3, 4, 4, 4, 4, 5, 5, 6, 6) more sts.

Join-up: Turn work to RS. Slip last st cast on back to LH needle, k2tog with first front st to join in round —126 (138, 146, 158, 170, 182, 194, 202, 214, 226) sts.

BODY

Begin working in stockinette stitch in the round. Work even until body measures 11¾ (12, 12¼, 12½, 12¾, 13, 13¼, 13½, 13¾, 14)" [30 (30.5, 31, 32, 32.5, 33, 33.5, 34.5, 35, 35.5) cm] from underarm, or desired depth to split hem. Break yarn.

HEMS

Hems are worked back and forth in rows.

Front hem

Remove beginning of round marker. Slip the first 5 (6, 7, 9, 11, 12, 14, 14, 16, 18) sts to RH needle. Join yarn, leaving a 10" [25 cm] tail.

Change to shorter US 10.5 [6.5 mm] circ.

Row 1: (RS) K53 (57, 59, 61, 63, 67, 69, 73, 75, 77) front hem sts. Turn work to WS.

Remaining 73 (81, 87, 97, 107, 115, 125, 129, 139, 149) sts will rest on longer circ while front hem is worked.

Row 2: K1, [p1, k1] to end.

Row 3: K1, [sl 1, p1] to last 2 sts, sl 1, k1.

Rep Rows 2 and 3 ten more times. Hem should measure 3" [7.5 cm]. Bind off front hem stitches in pattern.

Back hem

With RS facing, join yarn, leaving a 10" [25 cm] tail.

Row 1: (RS) Knit. Turn work to WS.

Row 2: K1, [p1, k1] to end.

Row 3: K1, [sl 1, p1] to last 2 sts, sl 1, k1.

Rep Rows 2 and 3 ten more times. Hem should measure 3" [7.5 cm]. Bind off all stitches in pattern.

Finish hem

Thread tail from start of front hem onto yarn needle. Reinforce separation point of front and back hems by whip-stitching them together with one or two stitches. Repeat for other side of hem. Weave in ends.

Neckband

With RS of back neck facing, attach yarn at right shoulder. With 24" [60 cm] long US 8 [5 mm] circ, pick up and knit 27 (27, 29, 31, 31, 33, 35, 35, 35, 37) sts at back neck, 16 (17, 18, 18, 18, 17, 18, 20, 21, 20) sts along left side of neckline, 21 (21, 23, 25, 25, 27, 29, 29, 29, 31) sts along front neckline, and 16 (17, 18, 18, 18, 17, 18, 20, 21, 20) more sts along right side of neckline. Pm for beginning of round—80 (82, 88, 92, 92, 94, 100, 104, 106, 108) sts.

Rnd 1: [Sl 1, p1] to end.

Rnd 2: [K1, p1] to end. Rep these two rnds two more times, then work Rnd 1 once more. Bind off all stitches in pattern.

SLEEVES

Note: Pick up stitches using US 8 [5 mm] needle, then transfer them to 16" [40 cm] long US 10.5 [6.5 mm] circ before beginning to work sleeve cap.

Place a removable stitch marker on front and back 1 (1⅛, 1¼, 1⅜, 1½, 1½, 1¾, 1¾, 1⅞, 2)" [2.5 (2.75, 3.25, 3.5, 3.75, 4, 4.25, 4.5, 4.75, 5) cm] away from the shoulder seam. Place a third marker at the center of the underarm. The marker to right of shoulder seam is **M-one**, to left of shoulder is **M-two**, at underarm is **M-three**.

Begin at **M-one**. Working just inside the column of knit sts on the edge of armhole, pick up and knit 10 (10, 12, 14, 14, 16, 18, 18, 20, 22) sts between **M-one** and **M-two**, pick up and knit 16 (17, 17, 17, 18, 18, 18, 19, 20, 21) sts between **M-two** and the cast-on sts at underarm, **pm**, pick up and knit 1 st in each of the 4 (4, 5, 6, 8, 8, 10, 10, 12, 12) cast-on sts before **M-three**, place unique marker for beginning of round, pick up and knit 1 st in each of the remaining 4 (4, 5, 6, 8, 8, 10, 10, 12, 12) cast-on sts at underarm, **pm**, pick up and knit 16 (17, 17, 17, 18, 18, 18, 19, 20, 21) more sts, ending at **M-one**—50 (52, 56, 60, 66, 68, 74, 76, 84, 88) sts.

Remove **M-one, M-two** and **M-three**.

Shape upper cap

When working the short rows that shape the sleeve caps, the wraps are not picked up; they are left in place and the wrapped stitch is worked in the normal fashion.

Short Row 1: (RS) K10 (10, 12, 14, 14, 16, 18, 18, 20, 22), w&t; (WS) p10 (10, 12, 14, 14, 16, 18, 18, 20, 22), w&t.

Short Row 2: (RS) Knit to prev wrapped st, knit wrapped st, sl 1 wyif, shift yarn to back, w&t; (WS) purl to prev wrapped st, purl wrapped st, sl 1 wyib, bring yarn to front, w&t.

Rep Short Row 2 twice more.

Shape mid cap

Next short row: (RS) Knit to prev wrapped st, knit wrapped st, w&t; (WS) purl to prev wrapped st, purl wrapped st, w&t.

Rep this row, working back and forth to build the sleeve cap, until 3 (3, 5, 5, 5, 5, 5, 7, 7) sts remain before each of the side markers that separate the underarm sts from the sleeve cap.

Shape lower cap

Remove side markers as you come to them.

Next short row: (RS) Knit to prev wrapped st, knit wrapped st, then wrap the next 2 sts together & turn; (WS) purl to prev wrapped st, purl wrapped st, then wrap the next 2 sts together & turn.

Next short row *dec row:* (RS) Knit to twin-wrapped sts, knit wrapped sts tog as one st, wrap 2 sts together & turn; (WS) purl to twin-wrapped sts, purl wrapped sts tog as one st, wrap 2 sts together & turn—2 sts decreased.

Rep the last row 0 (0, 1, 1, 1, 1, 1, 1, 2, 2) more times.

Next short row *dec row:* (RS) Knit to twin-wrapped sts, knit wrapped sts tog as one st, wrap next single st & turn; (WS) purl to twin-wrapped sts, purl wrapped sts tog as one st, wrap next single st & turn—46 (48, 50, 54, 60, 62, 68, 70, 76, 80) sts.

Last row *dec row:* (RS) Knit to prev wrapped st, k2tog-tbl with next st, k1 (1, 2, 3, 5, 5, 7, 7, 9, 9)—45 (47, 49, 53, 59, 61, 67, 69, 75, 79) sts.

Work sleeve in the round

Rnd 1 *dec rnd:* K1 (1, 2, 3, 5, 5, 7, 7, 9, 9), k2tog with remaining wrapped st, knit to end of round—44 (46, 48, 52, 58, 60, 66, 68, 74, 78) sts.

Next 2 rnds: Knit.

Change to preferred needle style for small circumference knitting in the round when necessary.

Next rnd *dec rnd:* K1, ssk, knit to last 3 sts, k2tog, k1—2 sts decreased.

Work *dec rnd* every 19th (15th, 15th, 13th, 11th, 11th, 10th, 10th, 7th, 7th) rnd 3 (3, 3, 4, 5, 5, 6, 6, 8, 9) more times, then work even until sleeve measures 10½ (11, 11, 11½, 11½, 12, 12, 12½, 12½, 13)" [26.5 (28, 28, 29, 29, 30.5, 30.5, 32, 32, 33) cm] from underarm, or desired length to cuff—36 (38, 40, 42, 46, 48, 52, 54, 56, 58) sts.

Work cuff

Change to US 10 [6 mm] needles.

Rnd 1: [P1, k1] to end.

Rnd 2: [P1, sl 1] to end.

Rep Rnds 1 and 2 six more times.

Change to US 9 [5.5 mm] needles.

Rep Rnds 1 and 2 until cuff measures 6" [15 cm], or desired length to wrist. Bind off all stitches loosely in pattern.

Finishing

Weave in all ends. Block sweater to measurements.

adjustments and fitting

making modifications

Very few of us can ever knit a sweater from a pattern without having (or wanting!) to make some kind of adjustment to it—after all, one of the best reasons for making your own garments is that you *can* customize them to suit your unique shape or style preferences.

Gauge is where it all begins. Even if all the dimensions on the pattern's schematic happen to be absolutely perfect for you, if your swatch shows that your row gauge is different from the pattern's, or that the stitch gauge is off by just a portion of a stitch, you'll want to adjust for it to be certain that your finished sweater fits as you intended.

If you've chosen your garment size based upon your cross-shoulder measurement, some modifications to the pattern's circumferential measurements may be needed. Maybe you'll want to modify the bust or hip circumference, or tweak the fit of the sleeves.

As for vertical adjustments, you may need to change the depth of the armhole to compensate for a change you'll be making to the bust circumference, or to adjust the sleeve fit. Since the patterns in this book are worked top-down, once you've joined fronts and back at the underarms, all the other vertical adjustments, such as the positioning of waist shaping increases and decreases, or changes to the overall length can usually be made on the fly.

So plan ahead, try on the garment frequently as it progresses, and use the information in this section to help create your perfect-fitting sweater.

knitting a gauge swatch

I know.

But here's the thing—your gauge swatch is your ally. That small square of knitting can tell you most of what you need to know about your sweater's chances for success. It's not just a means of verifying that you've achieved the pattern's stitch and row gauge—your swatch will also allow you to preview your fabric and decide if you're happy with it before you commit time, resources and your good will to the project.

When you swatch, you get to know the 'hand' of the knitted fabric—is it too drapey? too firm? how's the stitch definition? Unsure about whether you'll like the fabric next to your skin? Tuck the swatch into your clothing and wear it around for a while. Will it pill the instant it's off the needles? Rub it vigorously against the leg of your jeans and you'll find out. And since even a solid color yarn can look quite different between the skein and the knitted fabric, you also get to see what the color you've selected looks like knitted up.

how to swatch

The bigger the swatch, the more reliable the information. That said, as long as your swatch is large enough that you can measure 4" [10 cm] of undistorted stitches in each direction, you're fine. Since stitches can be a little wobbly at the edge

of the swatch, or where you change from one stitch pattern to another, make a square that's big enough to measure that distance without the ruler touching any edge stitches.

Use the stitch pattern given in the pattern's gauge statement. For the sweaters in this book, that's stockinette. The swatch instructions on page 102 will work for all of them.

Once you've completed your swatch, take a minute to measure it edge-to-edge in both directions. Make a note of the overall dimensions *before* you wet-block it. Keeping notes on the before and after measurements will allow you to predict what will happen when you wash and block your garment.

washing and blocking

Fill a sink with lukewarm water and a little wool wash, submerge the swatch, and let it soak for at least 20 minutes. Drain the sink, gently squeeze out the excess water, then roll the swatch in a towel and press out as much moisture as you can.

Lay your swatch on a flat surface, patting it into shape. Use pins to square up the edges if you like, but remove them before the swatch is dry. Allow your swatch to dry fully before measuring gauge. Use a hair dryer set on low and held well away from the swatch to speed things up if you really, really can't wait.

stockinette gauge swatch

Loosely cast on 34 stitches, using the long-tail cast-on. Work three rows in garter stitch, then continue as follows:

Row 1: (RS) Knit.

Row 2: K2, purl to last 2 sts, k2.

Repeat Rows 1 and 2 until the swatch measures at least 5" [12.5 cm] from the garter stitch band at bottom.

Work three rows in garter stitch, then bind off all stitches loosely.

Tip: Once you've worked a few rows past the garter edging, if you'd like to mark your needle size on the swatch, begin working 2 extra knit stitches at the start of the wrong side rows as follows:

Marker row: (WS) K4, purl to last 2 sts, k2.

Work the marker row in place of Row 2 as many times as the size number of your needle. If you need to indicate a quarter size, say for a 3.25 mm needle, knit 5 stitches at the beginning of the final marker row; for a half size, knit 6. Resume working Row 2 until the swatch reaches the desired length. Bind off loosely.

measuring gauge

When it's dry, shake out your swatch, and lay it flat on a table. A hard surface is best, because if you are tempted to smooth your stitches out, they will slide back to their actual shape when you stop smoothing.

First, re-measure the overall, edge-to-edge dimensions, and make a note of them. Next comes the Zen-mind exercise: Forget that you are looking for any specific stitch and row count, and just measure the swatch you see.

Beginning a few stitches in from the garter stitch edge, place a fine straight pin between two stitches. Take care not to distort the fabric. Align one

of the major division marks of your ruler with the pin, then place a second pin exactly 4" [10.16 cm] away from the first, even if this measurement falls partially within a stitch.

Count up the number of stitches—and any fraction of a stitch—between the two pins and write it down. Repeat the exercise at a couple of points on your swatch. You may notice a difference between the beginning of your swatch where you were focused on the task, and the end where you've relaxed a bit. If so, the later measurement is probably the more accurate one.

Turn your swatch 90°, and repeat the pinning and measuring process for the row gauge. Check the

gauge at a couple of points across the swatch. Write down your measurements.

evaluating your findings

First compare the overall dimensions of the un-blocked and blocked swatch. If you see a difference in these measurements, you can anticipate a change between the pre- and post-blocking states of your garment too.

Stitch gauge Now compare your swatch's stitch gauge to the pattern's stitch gauge. If there's a difference between the two, change needle sizes and work a new swatch. If you have more stitches per 4" [10 cm] than the pattern's gauge, use a larger needle; if fewer, try a smaller one.

A half stitch difference can often be made up by going up or down one needle size. For a full stitch difference, try going up or down two needle sizes.

It's tempting to try to conserve yarn by pulling out your old swatch and knitting the new one with the same yarn—but don't. Yarn that has been washed and blocked will be kinked, and will not produce an accurate gauge swatch. Plus, it's useful to be able to compare your new swatch to the previous one. If you need those few yards at the end of your project, you can always recover the swatch yarn then.

If you've tried changing needle sizes and the closest you can get to the pattern's stitch gauge is still a little bit off, see page 104 for advice on making gauge adjustments.

Row gauge Once you've found the stitch gauge that will work for your chosen pattern, it's tempting to just cast on. But there is another dimension to your swatch that is equally important to check, and that's row gauge.

Why does it matter? A difference in row gauge can cause parts of the garment to be longer or shorter than they were intended to be. This can be tragic for armholes, in particular. Luckily, it's fairly easy to compensate for row gauge differences—if you plan ahead. See page 104 for further advice.

a word on metric measurements and swatching

The convention used for the patterns in this book is to round imperial measurements to the nearest quarter-inch, and metric measurements to the nearest half-centimeter.

All of the metric measurements given in the patterns and schematics are calculated directly from the stitch and row counts for each size—not from the already-rounded inch measurements. But for knitters who use the metric system, the place where rounding can make things a little fuzzy is in the gauge statement, which is written as:

x number of stitches = 4" [10 cm]

In reality, 4" = 10.16 cm. At some gauges, this could add up to as much as half a stitch difference. So to be absolutely precise when measuring gauge for these designs, use 10.16 cm, or use a ruler with imperial markings, and measure over 4".

adjusting for gauge differences

Small differences between your gauge and the pattern's might at first seem inconsequential, but when they are multiplied out over the length and breadth of the garment, those little variations can mean the difference between a sweater that fits as you intended it, and one that does not. Here's how to evaluate and correct for those differences.

stitch gauge differences

If you've swatched, tried changing needle sizes, and the closest you can get to the pattern's stitch gauge is still a little ways off—but you like the fabric you are getting—you can use some simple math to determine whether the size you've chosen will still work for you.

First, take the stitch gauge from your swatch, and divide it by the unit of measurement you are using. If inches, divide by 4; if centimeters, by 10. This number is your *stitches per inch/cm*.

Say you're making Sans Serif in the 42¼" [107.5 cm] bust size. It has a finished shoulder width of 14½" [37 cm]. The stitch gauge for the bodice of the pattern is 17 stitches = 4" [10 cm] in stockinette stitch, but you're getting 17½ stitches = 4" [10 cm]. Divide by 4 [or 10] and you've got 4⅜ stitches per inch, or 1.75 stitches per cm.

Now look at your pattern and find the stitch count for the full cross-shoulder width for your size. This will be the stitch count after the shoulder pieces are joined. Subtract the 2 selvedge stitches from that number. This is your *shoulder stitch count*.

64 − 2 = 62 shoulder stitches

Divide the *shoulder stitch count* by the *stitches per inch/cm*. This will give you the new cross-shoulder width of your sweater, if you were to cast on at that gauge. Compare this number to your actual cross-shoulder measurement to find out if the pattern size/gauge combination will work.

62 ÷ 4.375 [or 1.75] = 14.17" [35.432 cm]

If the new size is too wide or too narrow for your actual cross-shoulder width, find the *shoulder stitch count* for the next size up or down from your chosen size and divide that number by your *stitches per inch/cm*. The next size larger is 66 stitches wide, including selvedge stitches.

66 − 2 = 64 shoulder stitches
64 ÷ 4.375 [or 1.75] = 14.63" [36.57 cm]

So in this case, using the starting numbers for the next size up would give you a shoulder width closer to the size you'd originally chosen to make.

This method will work well when there is a small difference between your stitch gauge and the specified gauge, but not all features of a sweater pattern will scale easily, so if you have a difference of a more than half a stitch, it is usually best to swatch again with another needle.

row gauge differences

Every knitter is different, and it can be a challenge to match both the stitch and row gauge specified in a pattern. In a top-down set-in sleeve design, row gauge is important for achieving the proper armhole depth. A seemingly small difference in row gauge can have a huge effect on the depth of the armhole, and in turn, the overall fit of the sweater, so it's important to take row gauge into account, at least to begin with.

Once the armholes are complete, the remainder of the sweater is knit to fit your own shape, and row gauge doesn't matter nearly as much.

You can easily adjust for a difference in row gauge by adding or subtracting rows from the upper part of the bodice—the part that's worked straight before beginning the underarm shaping.

Say you're making Sans Serif in the 38½" [98 cm] bust size. You're getting the correct stitch gauge, but the pattern calls for 26 rows over 4" [10 cm] and you're getting only 23. That's a difference of about 13%.

At first glance this may not seem like a lot, but if you don't correct for it, the 8" [20.5 cm] deep armhole you think you are knitting will end up more than 9" [23 cm] deep. That's enough to significantly change the fit of your sweater's bodice and sleeves. Some simple arithmetic will help us out.

To calculate the number of rows you'll need to maintain the correct armhole depth, divide your swatch's row gauge by the pattern's gauge. This will give you the *adjustment factor*.

23 ÷ 26 = .885 adjustment factor

Next, add up the total number of rows for the armhole, then subtract the number of short rows worked for shoulder shaping.

For this size this is 1 (cast on) + 9 (set-up row to yarn marker) + 36 (yarn marker to shaping) + 12 (underarm shaping rows) = 58, minus 6 (short rows) = 52 total rows for the armhole.

Multiply the total rows in the armhole by the adjustment factor.

52 x .885 = 46.02

Round to the closest even number. When in doubt, round down.

46.02 = 46

Subtract the new number from the total rows.

52-46 = 6

So, in this case, you'd begin the underarm shaping 6 rows higher than the pattern says to, working 30 rows after the yarn marker, rather than 36.

If your row gauge is tighter than the pattern's, it still works the same way. You divide your gauge by the pattern's, but your adjustment factor will be greater than 1, so you'll be adding rows before beginning the underarm shaping rather than subtracting them.

Either way, remember to adjust by the same number of rows on the front(s) as you do on the back.

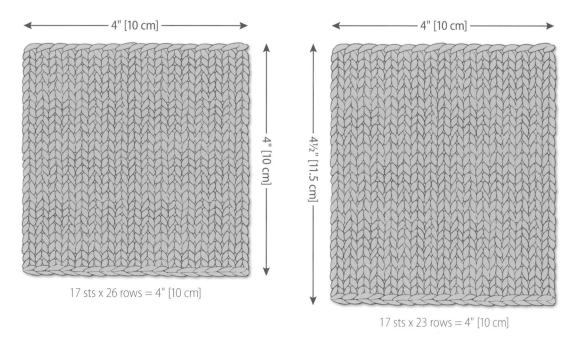

17 sts x 26 rows = 4" [10 cm]

17 sts x 23 rows = 4" [10 cm]

Figure 12. Same stitch gauge, different row gauge

adjusting fit

So you've chosen your sweater size based on your cross-shoulder measurement, as explained on page 24. You've compared your bust, waist, hip and upper arm measurements to the pattern's schematic and noted any differences. You've checked the overall length of the body and sleeves, and decided whether alterations are needed. (And of course, you've made any necessary adjustments for a difference in gauge, too!) Let's look at customizing the fit of your sweater, starting from the top.

shoulder slope adjustments

The sweaters in this book all begin with a few short rows to shape the garment to the body's natural shoulder slope. Although the angle of this slope varies from person to person, for most people, the pattern instructions will be just fine. For those who have very straight shoulders, or a very pronounced slope, some adjustment of this angle may be desired.

• For a flatter shoulder slope, you can eliminate the short row shaping altogether, or work fewer short rows than the pattern calls for by increasing the number of stitches worked beyond the previous turn.

• To steepen the shoulder slope, work more short rows by decreasing the number of stitches worked beyond the previous turn.

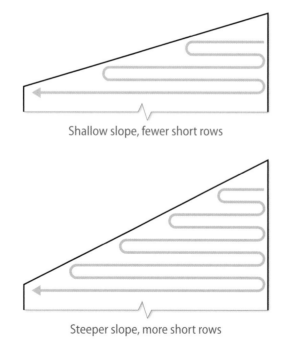

Shallow slope, fewer short rows

Steeper slope, more short rows

Figure 13. Shoulder slope angles

Note that changing the shoulder slope of the garment will not affect the armhole depth, since the shoulder shaping all takes place before the armhole is worked.

bust circumference alterations

After the shoulder shaping is complete, both the back and the fronts are worked straight for a distance, then gradual increases are made and stitches cast on to shape the underarm curve. When the fronts and back are joined, additional stitches are cast on between them to form the bottom of the underarm.

Once the fronts and back have been joined in one piece, the number of stitches you have on the needles will be the full stitch count for your pattern's bust circumference—less the width of any front bands, of course.

Put another way, all the stitches that make up the difference in width between the upper bodice of the sweater and the desired bust circumference are added to the body during the shaping of the underarms and joining of fronts to back—so that's where any adjustment of the bust circumference will take place.

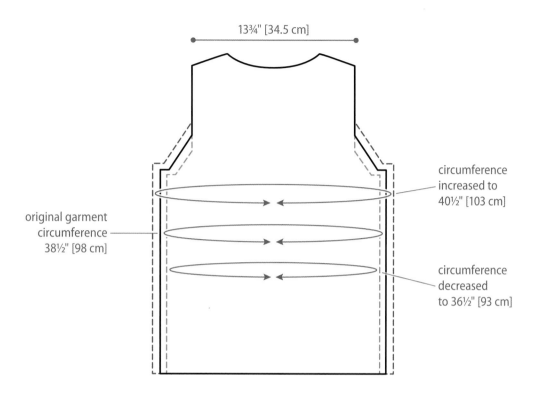

13¾" [34.5 cm]

original garment
circumference
38½" [98 cm]

circumference
increased to
40½" [103 cm]

circumference
decreased
to 36½" [93 cm]

Figure 14. Modifying the bust circumference only; shoulder width stays the same

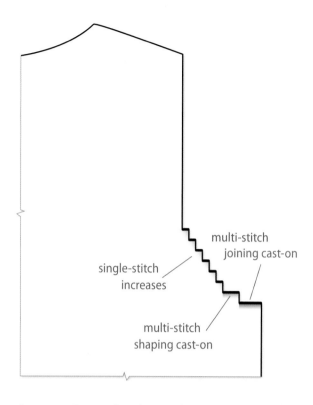

multi-stitch
joining cast-on

single-stitch
increases

multi-stitch
shaping cast-on

Figure 15. Types of underarm shaping increases

Working extra increases while shaping the underarms will increase the sweater's overall bust circumference; working fewer will decrease it. Let's look at an example:

Say you're making Sans Serif. You've chosen the 38½" [98 cm] size because that's the one that most closely matches your shoulder width. Your actual bust measurement is 40½" [103 cm], and you'd like to have the sweater fit with zero ease through the bust—so you know that you'll need

to add 2" [5 cm] worth of stitches to the total circumference of the garment. The pattern's stitch gauge is 17 sts = 4" [10 cm], or 4¼ sts = 1" [2.5 cm].

2" x 4¼ sts per inch = 8½ sts needed.

Round this to the closest even number (8), then divide by 2, allocating 4 extra stitches to each armhole: 2 on the front, and 2 on the back. If instead you wanted a bust circumference that was 2" [5 cm] smaller, you'd work 4 fewer increases at each armhole.

Underarm shaping increases

In the course of shaping the underarms, three types of increases are used. These are:

• Single stitch increases, worked a few stitches in from the edge, that create a gradual taper along the sides of the armhole.

• Multiple stitches cast on to create the curved shape of the bottom of the armhole.

• Multiple stitches cast on at the bottom of the underarm when joining fronts and back.

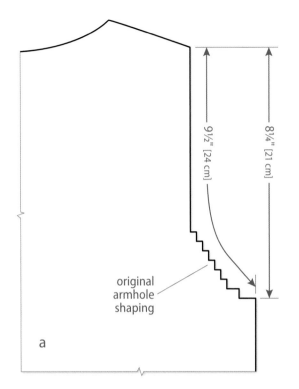

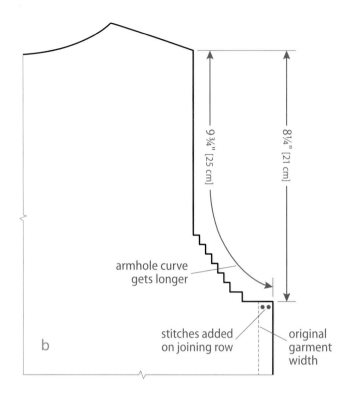

Figure 16. Effect of increases to the bust circumference on the length of the armhole curve

armhole depth considerations

The ideal armhole will fit as close to the underarm as is possible without binding or chafing. If the sweater is meant to be worn over other garments, a little extra ease is figured in, but because the size of the armhole determines the starting circumference of the sleeve, a closer fit is usually desirable.

On a pattern's schematic the armhole measurement that's normally given is the depth, measured vertically, from shoulder to underarm—but this measurement does not tell the whole story. If you lay a garment flat and look at the shape of the armhole, you can see that the measurement that really determines the sleeve circumference is the overall length of the armhole curve.

Two garments can have exactly the same armhole depth measured vertically, but if the armholes are wider on one of them, more stitches will need to be picked up for the sleeve to fit into that armhole without puckering.

By comparing the armhole curves in Figures 16a and b above, you'll see that if you adjust the bust circumference by adding stitches to the underarm cast-on, you will also lengthen the armhole curve, increasing the armhole's overall circumference. This, in turn, will affect the circumference of the sleeve at the upper arm.

If you want a sleeve that's larger than the measurement given on the pattern's schematic, this might be fine. But if you make changes to

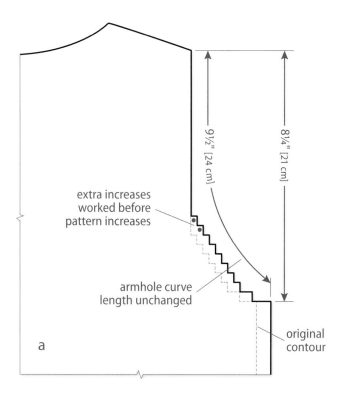

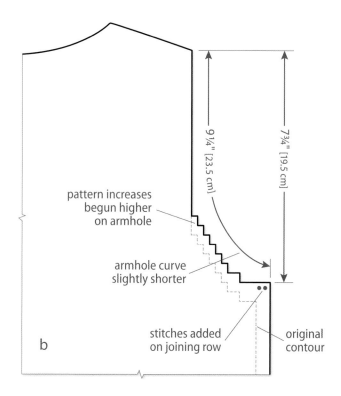

Figure 17. Adjusting the position of the shaping to maintain the length of the armhole curve

the width of the body of a sweater and want to maintain the upper arm measurement that is shown for that size, you will need to adjust the depth of the armhole so that the overall length of the armhole curve remains roughly the same as the original.

The place where stitches are added or subtracted can also affect circumference of the sleeve. Since stitches cast on at the underarm are picked up one-for-one, any stitches added to the shaping

cast-ons or to the underarm joining cast-on will later get picked up, increasing the starting stitch count for the sleeve.

If instead you add single-stitch increases, working them before of the pattern's increases, the overall length of the armhole curve stays virtually the same, as does the starting stitch count (Figure 17a). Where possible, this is the preferred way to make smaller increases to the bust circumference.

To maintain the armhole circumference given in the pattern while increasing the bust circumference, the shaping must begin higher up on the bodice (Figure 17b). Since the shaping increases are worked on the right side rows only, each increase that's added actually accounts for two rows.

Let's say you're going to add 2 single-stitch increases to each side of the armhole.

2 increases x 2 rows per increase = 4 rows

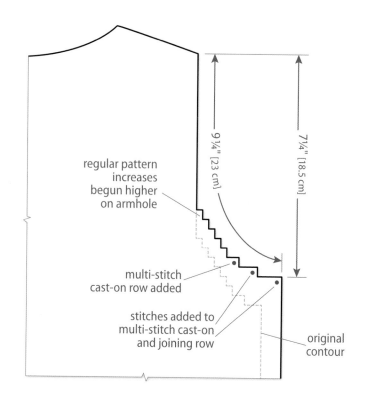

regular pattern
increases
begun higher
on armhole

9¼" [23 cm]

7¼" [18.5 cm]

multi-stitch
cast-on row added

stitches added to
multi-stitch cast-on
and joining row

original
contour

Figure 18. Adjusting the position of the shaping to maintain the length of the armhole curve

You'll begin the underarm shaping 4 rows higher on the armhole. So if the instructions for your size say to begin the underarm shaping after 36 rows have been worked, you'd start increasing after 32 rows. If you adjust the number of cast-on stitches, either as a multi-stitch shaping cast-on, or by adding stitches to the joining row it works the same way. If you add 2 stitches to each side of the joining cast-on (Figure 16b), again, you'd begin the underarm shaping 4 rows higher. Note

that this will actually result in an armhole curve that is slightly shorter than the original, but the number of stitches that will be picked up around the armhole is the same, so the sleeve circumference will be unchanged.

Bear in mind that adjustments made to the depth of the armhole must be done symmetrically—if you begin the shaping higher up on the back of the sweater, you'll need to begin it at the same point on the fronts, so that the armhole

depth is the same front and back. Plotting the shaping out on graph paper can be very helpful.

Larger bust adjustments

If you are just adding a few stitches to the circumference, and can fit them in as single-stitch increases ahead of the pattern's increases, that's usually best, since it won't affect the depth of the armhole. But if you were to add a lot of stitches to the garment this way it might cause the shaping to begin too close to the shoulder, and it would give you an armhole that was quite narrow at the bottom relative to its width.

When you have more than 2" [5 cm] to add to the total bust circumference, it's better to add some stitches to the shaping cast-on rows, the joining cast-on row, or even add another multi-stitch shaping cast-on row (Figure 18).

Ideally the armhole shaping should begin approximately where your upper bust circumference begins to increase. As a rule of thumb, it's best to keep the shaping rows to less than 40% of the original vertical armhole measurement. So if the armhole depth measurement given on the schematic for your size is 8½" [21.5 cm], the shaping would not begin until the armhole measures at least 5" [13 cm] from the shoulder seam. If you make a larger bust adjustment and adjust the armhole depth to match, see 'Adjusting cap depth', page 112.

sweater body adjustments

Working from the top, you can try on your growing sweater as often as you like and make assessments about the fit and the length as you go.

Waist shaping modifications are therefore simple—just work more (or fewer) shaping rows at the underbust and hips to achieve your desired fit. In most cases, since you are taking your shaping cues from the points where your body actually changes shape, there aren't really any calculations that you'll need to make.

If you are knitting a garment with patterning at the hem (like Underwood), it may be best to make your adjustments so that the final stitch count is that of the next size larger or smaller, so that you can use the pattern instructions for that size, and not have to tinker with the stitch pattern.

And if the final stitch count is a multiple of some number—say a four- or eight-stitch repeat for ribbing—you'll need to add or subtract stitches in that same pattern multiple.

Keep in mind also, that although the waist shaping instructions are written symmetrically in the pattern, they don't necessarily have to be worked that way. You can shape the front or back alone, or begin the hip increases later on the back than on the front if that suits your shape better, or adjust their vertical spacing—it's up to you.

sleeve cap adjustments

Since stitches are picked up at specific rates for different parts of the sleeve cap, the total number of stitches picked up is determined, mainly, by the circumference of the armhole. Sometimes you'll just wind up with the wrong number of stitches for your desired sleeve circumference. What can you do if this is just going to result in a sleeve that will be too big at the upper arm?

• If you are able to plan ahead, the best solution is to adjust the length of the armhole curve, as described under 'Armhole depth considerations' (starting on page 108), by subtracting a few rows from the portion of the upper bodice that is worked straight.

• You can whittle away a few extra stitches in the lower cap area by working an additional pair or two of twin-wrap decreases. Just keep the total number of stitches that will be decreased in the lower cap to less than 15% of the sleeve stitches picked up.

• If these remedies are not quite enough, you can also eliminate a few extra stitches by working additional sleeve decrease rounds immediately after the sleeve is joined in the round.

Say you're making Sans Serif in the 42¼" [107.5 cm] size, and you want to keep the bust circumference as written. The upper arm circumference given in the pattern is 15¼" [39 cm], but you'd prefer an upper arm measurement of 14¼" [36 cm], or 1" [2.5 cm] smaller.

1" x 4¼ stitches per inch = 4¼ stitches. Round this to the closest even number, and you'll need 4 fewer stitches for each sleeve, or 2 stitches less for each side of the sleeve. The preferred way to adjust for this is to begin the armhole shaping 4 rows higher on the body—2 rows for each stitch you want to eliminate. But if the body of the sweater is already complete, the best solution is to add another pair of twin-wrap decreases to the lower cap area, and work a decrease round as soon as you begin working in the round.

If instead you needed a slightly larger sleeve circumference, you could:

• Increase the armhole depth by adding a few rows to the part of the upper bodice that is worked straight.

• Work fewer twin-wrap decreases in the lower cap shaping.

• Skip the first set of decreases that would normally be worked just after joining the sleeve in the round.

• If the body of the sweater is complete, but the armhole is too tight, try picking up stitches one row lower in the bottom of the underarm, and pick up one more on each side of the armhole.

Upper cap fullness

If you are working at a loose gauge, or if the curve of your shoulders is pronounced, it may be desirable to have a little more fabric in the upper cap. In this case, pick up all of the available upper cap stitches, (one stitch for each row, rather than the 85–90% that the pattern calls for), then work extra twin-wrap decreases when you shape the lower cap to get back to your desired stitch count for the upper arm.

cap depth considerations

In a top-down set-in sleeve, the depth of the sleeve cap is determined by the number of short rows that are worked before the sleeve is joined in the round. The more rows worked, the longer the cap becomes, and the more steeply the sleeve angles downward.

A shallower cap depth is used in sweaters designed to fit with more than a couple of inches of positive ease in the body, such as Clarendon, and in garments meant for active outdoor wear.

These will have a wider and shallower armhole compared to a classic-fitting sweater. The shallow armhole means that there are fewer rows available between the upper cap and the lower cap—hence a shorter sleeve cap depth—so the sleeve will join the body at a more open angle.

Adjusting cap depth

If you add more than 2" [5 cm] to the circumference of your sweater and reduce the armhole depth to compensate you will likely want to shorten the sleeve cap depth as well.

To shorten the cap, work an extra row or two of the upper cap shaping. Since each row is worked to one stitch beyond the previous wrap, each upper cap short row pair consumes an additional row. Working just a few extra rows in this fashion will make the angle of the sleeve less acute.

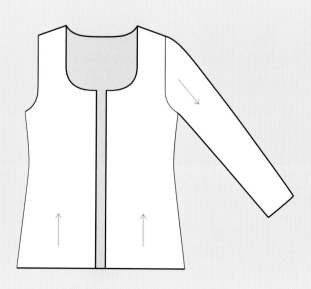

bottom up, top down

What if you happen to be knitting a set-in sleeve sweater that's worked from the bottom up, and would prefer to knit the sleeves top down? Unless you have a stitch motif that is directional, or some complicated shaping such as pleats that would be difficult to reverse, it's pretty straightforward to adapt most sleeves to be worked from the top.

When the body of the sweater is complete, pick up sleeve stitches around the armhole using the rates described on page 22. To calculate the number of stitches to decrease in the lower cap, multiply your desired upper arm circumference, including ease, by your stitch gauge, (or refer to your pattern for its upper arm stitch count). Subtract that number from the number of stitches picked up, then subtract the two stitches that are decreased when joining in the round. The remainder is the number of stitches you'll need to decrease before joining in the round.

If the number of decreases needed is more than 15% of the stitches picked up, save a few decreases to be worked soon after you join in the round.

abbreviations

approx	approximately	**LH**	left hand	**rnd(s)**	round(s)
CO	cast on	**LLI**	left lifted increase	**RS**	right side
circ	circular needle	**m1**	make 1	**sl**	slip
cm	centimeter(s)	**m1L**	make 1 left	**sl m**	slip marker
dec	decrease	**m1p**	make 1 purl	**sl-tbl**	slip through the back loop
dpn(s)	double-pointed needle(s)	**m1R**	make 1 right	**ssk**	slip, slip, knit
est	establish(ed)	**mm**	millimeter(s)	**sssk**	slip, slip, slip, knit
g	gram(s)	**p**	purl	**st(s)**	stitch(es)
inc	increase	**p2tog**	purl 2 together	**tbl**	through the back loop
k	knit	**patt(s)**	pattern(s)	**tog**	together
k2tog	knit 2 together	**pfb**	purl front and back	**w&t**	wrap and turn
k2tog-tbl	knit 2 together through the back loops	**pfkb**	purl front, knit back	**wyib**	with yarn in back
		pm	place marker	**wyif**	with yarn in front
k3tog	knit 3 together	**prev**	previous(ly)	**WS**	wrong side
kfb	knit front and back	**rep**	repeat; repeating	**yd**	yard(s)
kfpb	knit front, purl back	**RLI**	right lifted increase	**yo**	yarn over

special techniques

cast-ons

Backwards loop cast-on: Wrap yarn around left thumb from front to back and secure in palm with other fingers. Insert right needle upward through strand on thumb. Slip loop from thumb onto needle, gently pulling yarn to tighten—1 stitch cast on.

Cable cast-on: Insert right needle tip between the first two stitches on left needle, wrap yarn as if to knit, pull loop through and place on left needle tip to form a new stitch—1 stitch cast on.

Knitted cast-on: Knit into first stitch on left needle and place resulting loop on left needle tip to form a new stitch—1 stitch cast on.

Purled cast-on: Purl into first stitch on left needle and place resulting loop on left needle tip to form a new stitch—1 stitch cast on.

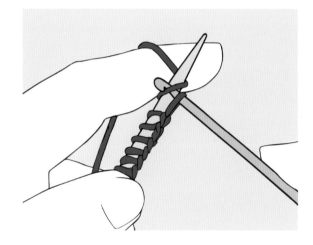

Provisional cast-on: Make a loose slip knot in the waste yarn, and place on crochet hook. Hold knitting needle in left hand and crochet hook in right. Let hook rest on top of needle with yarn hanging at right side. * Bring yarn, from right to left, behind knitting needle, over the top of both needle and crochet hook, and around again to back. With crochet hook, pull loop through existing loop on hook—1 stitch cast onto needle.

Repeat from * until required number of stitches has been cast on, then chain a few more stitches off the needle. Break waste yarn and pull through last loop. This tail serves as a reminder of which end to unravel from later.

decreases

k2tog: Knit two stitches together—1 stitch decreased (right-slanting).

k3tog: Knit three stitches together—2 stitches decreased (right-slanting).

k2tog-tbl: Knit two stitches together through the back loops—1 stitch decreased (left-slanting).

p2tog: Purl two stitches together—1 stitch decreased.

ssk (slip, slip, knit): Slip the next two stitches one at a time to right needle as if to knit; return them to the left needle in turned position and knit them together through the back loops—1 stitch decreased (left-slanting).

sssk (slip, slip, slip, knit): Slip the next three stitches one at a time to right needle as if to knit; return them to the left needle in turned position and knit them together through the back loops—2 stitches decreased (left-slanting).

increases

kfb (knit front and back): Knit into the next stitch, then without removing stitch from needle, knit into the back loop—1 stitch increased.

kfpb (knit front, purl back): Knit into the next stitch, then without removing stitch from needle, bring yarn to the front between needles and purl into the back loop—1 stitch increased.

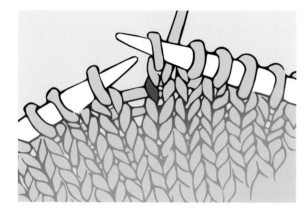

LLI (left lifted increase): With left needle, pick up the left leg of the stitch two stitches below the stitch just worked on your right needle and knit into it—1 stitch increased.

m1 (make 1): See m1R.

m1L (make 1 left): Insert left needle tip, from front to back, under the strand of yarn running between the next stitch on left needle and last stitch on right needle; knit strand through the back loop—1 stitch increased.

m1R (make 1 right): Insert left needle tip, from back to front, under the strand of yarn running between the next stitch on left needle and last stitch on right needle; knit strand through the front loop—1 stitch increased.

m1p (make 1 purl): Insert left needle tip, from front to back, under the strand of yarn running between the next stitch on left needle and last stitch on right needle; purl strand through the back loop—1 stitch increased.

pfb (purl front and back): Purl into the next stitch, then without removing stitch from needle, purl into the back loop—1 stitch increased.

pfkb (purl front, knit back): Purl into the next stitch, then without removing stitch from needle, take yarn to back between needles and knit into the back loop—1 stitch increased.

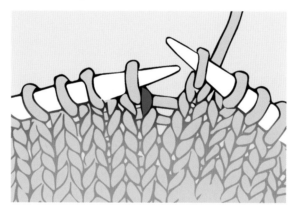

RLI (right lifted increase): With right needle, pick up the right leg of the stitch below the next stitch on left needle, place on left needle and knit into it—1 stitch increased.

yo (yarn over): Bring yarn between needles to the front, then over right needle to back, ready to knit the next stitch—1 stitch increased.

short rows

See page 68.

twisted stitches

k-tbl: Knit stitch through the back loop to twist.

p-tbl: Purl stitch through the back loop to twist.

sl-tbl (slip through the back loop): With yarn in back, slip stitch as if to purl through the back loop. This operation pre-twists a stitch that will be worked into a decrease on the next round.

links to tutorials

Cable and knitted cast-ons
https://vimeo.com/122460780

Provisional cast-on
https://vimeo.com/91476816

Right and left lifted increases
https://vimeo.com/122746103

Seaming garter stitch
https://vimeo.com/128878261

Wrap-and-turn short rows
https://vimeo.com/128883334

about elizabeth

Elizabeth Doherty lives and designs and rides her bike in California's Sierra Nevada. She has a background in fine art and graphic design, and long experience in sewing tailored garments. Her knitting designs have been published by Quince & Company, Brooklyn Tweed and Twist Collective.

www.bluebeestudio.com

about quince & company

Quince & Company makes beautiful yarns in natural fibers. We spin our yarns primarily in New England from wool sourced from American sheep. We began in 2010 with four classic wool yarns in weights from sport to chunky, each dyed in 37 colors. Today we make nine different yarns in the United States and import two organic linen yarns from Italy. We ship our yarns all over the world—from Tasmania to Korea to Brazil.

Find out more about us at www.quinceandco.com.

acknowledgments

My profound thanks to Pam Allen for pushing me to delve deeper into the mysteries of the sleeve cap; and for her lovely photographs; but most of all for her generous support and encouragement throughout this journey. Thanks, also, to the fantastic Quince team, Ryan FitzGerald, Jerusha Robinson, Dawn Catanzaro and Adi Kehoe for all their invaluable help.

Huge thanks to Bristol Ivy for her editing assistance; to Julia Trice, Trisha Harvey, and Barbara Shaw for their thoughtful feedback; to Taylor Sikes with Port City Models & Talent, and to Erica Snow for modeling the sweaters; and to sample knitters Christen Mamenko and Erin Birnel for their beautiful, beautiful work.

To my husband Adrian, who, through all the many months I spent working on this book, made sure that the cats and I got fed, read and reread the manuscript, and never, ever, sighed when I mentioned set-in sleeves (again), my love and gratitude.

And to my parents, who fostered in me—and my three engineer brothers—a shared fascination with how things work by dragging us on innumerable obligatory family field trips to mills, farms, quarries, workshops and factories all over the country. Thanks Mom and Dad, we loved it all, even the yucky parts.